Praise for *The One Jesus Loves*

"Robert Crosby h[...]esus; he's lived it. This grace is like a [...] we go, the more healing we find. T[...]

—[Jo]hn Ortberg, senior pastor
of Menlo Park Presbyterian
Church, and author of *Who
Is This Man?*

"Many authors ask, 'Do you know Jesus?' Bob Crosby dares to ask the more difficult question, 'How close are you to Jesus?' While grace allows us to know Christ, only a persistent and faithful pursuit results in closeness. This book describes Jesus' friendship circles, and the way to closer connection."

—Marshall Shelley, vice
president, *Christianity Today*

"After reading *The One Jesus Loves*, readers will not only understand how to deepen their personal relationships with God by drawing closer into His 'circle of intimacy,' but they will also see how becoming a closer follower of Christ can change every other relationship in their lives for the better."

—Mark Batterson, *New York
Times* best-selling author
of *The Circle Maker* and
Lead Pastor of National
Community Church

"The apostle Paul gave voice to the deepest desire of every sincere Christian when he wrote in Philippians 3:10, 'That I may know Him.' Intimacy with Christ is the goal of each growing believer. Robert C. Crosby's book *The One Jesus Loves* explores the meaning and possibility of nearness to Christ and directs readers toward this noble aspiration with biblical and practical guidance. I heartily recommend it to all Christ-followers."

—Mark L. Williams, general
overseer, Church of God,
Cleveland, Tennessee

"*The One Jesus Loves* is a serious reflection on an age-old conversation about the character of God. Our affirmation of God's character may start with His transcendent qualities and therefore make pronouncements like God is everywhere and is all powerful! But human curiosity also wonders if God is here (right now) and if God can do everything, can He do anything in particular in my life? Crosby affirms that salvation is an unconditional gift of God's grace, but some intimacies with God come only with relentless pursuit of Him. This book is all about Crosby's admonition that followers of Jesus refuse to follow at a distance; if you're not moving closer, you're moving away!"

—Byron D. Klaus, president,
Assemblies of God
Theological Seminary

"Crosby has hit another home run with *The One Jesus Loves*. This is required reading for those individuals desiring an intimate relationship with Jesus Christ. As we move closer to Christ, the greater the joy. After reading this book, you will understand how *The One Jesus Loves* experiences genuine intimacy with God."

—Robert E. Cooley, president
emeritus, Gordon-Conwell
Theological Seminary

"This subject is one that I've pondered for years. How do I experience a deeper intimacy with God? How can I make my faith more than a dutiful habit or a set of boundaries? In this book, Robert Crosby simply communicates how to do just that. As I read it, I saw how people over the centuries have embraced their Maker and joined His inner-circle. I plan to join them and hope this book helps you do the same."

—Dr. Tim Elmore, president of
GrowingLeaders.com

"*The One Jesus Loves* will inspire, teach, and encourage you to get closer to God. As Robert C. writes, 'There is a difference between being loved by someone and being in a love relationship.' If you want to cross the threshold of simply being loved by Jesus, as one of the 5,000, to being in a deeper relationship with Him, then this book is for you. Jesus is on the move, pursuing a closer relationship with us. *The One Jesus Loves* will help you discover the principles and actions the disciples took to become near His heart. This book will show you that we can all become 'the one Jesus loves.'"

— Guillermo J. Aguayo, senior
pastor, www.lacasadelpadre
.com

"Jesus Christ calls us out of the crowds and into ever-increasing intimacy with himself. In *The One Jesus Loves*, Robert Crosby shows us how that call moves us through six circles of relationship. It is an excellent resource on following Jesus, and I enthusiastically recommend it."

— Dr. George O. Wood, general
superintendent, Assemblies
of God, USA

"In *The One Jesus Loves*, Robert Crosby empowers the reader with a biblical prescription where complacent faith experiences are replaced with an intimate transformative relationship with Christ. By studying biblical truth from those closest to Christ when he walked on earth, Robert describes a catalytic journey where we can occupy space in God's 'inner circle.'"

— Rev. Samuel Rodriguez,
president, NHCLC,
Hispanic Evangelical
Association

"Dr. Robert Crosby has crafted a detailed, inspired guide to the daily pursuit of drawing closer to God that is unlike anything I have ever read before. By examining the lives and practices of Jesus' early followers, he illuminates the deep mystery and wonderful satisfaction that comes from an intimate relationship with Jesus Christ. Grace is freely given, but to truly know God requires a dedicated life of searching, each day revealing more clearly and beautifully His divine nature. *The One Jesus Loves* will challenge you, enlighten you, and fulfill you in such a powerful way that is sure to change your life and strengthen your faith. I would highly recommend this book to believers new and old who are wanting to take their walk with Christ to the next step and satisfy the deepest desires of their soul."

— Pastor Matthew Barnett,
cofounder of the Dream
Center

"Robert Crosby has written this wonderful book so that we will not settle for a saving relationship with God, but go on to a deep and personal one. When it comes to the intentions of our faith, better than insight is intimacy."

— Dr. Joel C. Hunter,
senior pastor of Northland—
A Church Distributed

The ONE
JESUS LOVES

ALSO BY ROBERT CROSBY

More than a Savior: When Jesus Calls You Friend

Living Life from the Soul

Conversation Starters for Parents and Kids

Conversation Starters for Couples (with Pamela Crosby)

The Teaming Church: Ministry in the Age of Collaboration

The ONE
JESUS LOVES

GRACE IS UNCONDITIONALLY GIVEN,
INTIMACY MUST BE RELENTLESSLY
PURSUED

ROBERT CROSBY

NELSON
BOOKS

An Imprint of Thomas Nelson

Published in Nashville, Tennessee, by Nelson Books, an imprint of Thomas Nelson. Nelson Books and Thomas Nelson are registered trademarks of HarperCollins Christian Publishing, Inc.

Thomas Nelson, Inc., titles may be purchased in bulk for educational, business, fund-raising, or sales promotional use. For information, please e-mail SpecialMarkets@ThomasNelson.com.

Unless otherwise noted, Scripture quotations are taken from the HOLY BIBLE, NEW INTERNATIONAL VERSION®, NIV®. Copyright © 1973, 1978, 1984, 2011 by Biblica, Inc.™ Used by permission of Zondervan. All rights reserved worldwide. www.zondervan.com

Scripture quotations marked ESV are from the ENGLISH STANDARD VERSION. © 2001 by Crossway Bibles, a division of Good News Publishers.

Scripture quotations marked NKJV are from the NEW KING JAMES VERSION®. © 1982 by Thomas Nelson, Inc. Used by permission. All rights reserved.

Scripture quotations marked NASB are from the NEW AMERICAN STANDARD BIBLE®, © The Lockman Foundation 1960, 1962, 1963, 1968, 1971, 1972, 1973, 1975, 1977, 1995. Used by permission.

Scripture quotations marked MSG are from *The Message* by Eugene H. Peterson. © 1993, 1994, 1995, 1996, 2000. Used by permission of NavPress Publishing Group. All rights reserved.

Scripture quotations marked KJV are from the King James Version.

Scripture quotations marked NLT are from the *Holy Bible*, New Living Translation. © 1996, 2004, 2007. Used by permission of Tyndale House Publishers, Inc., Wheaton, Illinois 60189. All rights reserved.

Scripture quotations marked CEV are from the CONTEMPORARY ENGLISH VERSION. © 1991 by the American Bible Society. Used by permission.

Scripture quotations marked GW are from GOD'S WORD Translation. Copyright © 1995 by God's Word to the Nations. Used by permission of Baker Publishing Group.

Scripture quotations marked NIRV are from the New International Reader's Version. Copyright © 1996, 1998 by Biblica, Inc.™ Used by permission of Zondervan. All rights reserved worldwide. www.zondervan.com

Scripture taken from the Common English Bible®, CEB® Copyright © 2010, 2011 by Common English Bible.™ Used by permission. All rights reserved worldwide. The "CEB" and "Common English Bible" trademarks are registered in the United States Patent and Trademark Office by Common English Bible. Use of either trademark requires the permission of Common English Bible.

Scripture quotations marked WEB are from the World English Bible, public domain.

Scripture quotations marked ISV are from the Holy Bible: International Standard Version®. Copyright © 2003 by The ISV Foundation. Used by permission of Davidson Press, Inc. ALL RIGHTS RESERVED INTERNATIONALLY.

Library of Congress Cataloging-in-Publication Data

Crosby, Robert.
 The one Jesus loves : grace is unconditionally given, intimacy is relentlessly pursued / Robert Crosby.
  pages cm
 Includes bibliographical references.
 ISBN 978-1-4002-0577-6
 1. Christian life. 2. Jesus Christ—Biography. I. Title.
 BV4501.3.C763 2014
 248.4—dc23   2013032950

Printed in the United States of America

HB 07.13.2018

That you may know him better.

—PAUL'S PRAYER, EPHESIANS 1:17

To Pamela, for not only being my partner in love and in life but also in the passionate pursuits of Jesus . . . for all times!

Contents

The Five Thousand: Enjoying the Gifts and Graces of Christ

Part 2: Encountering Christ, the Lord

The Seventy: Serving the Purposes of Christ

The Twelve: Following the Call of Christ

CONTENTS

Part 3: Knowing Christ, the Friend

The Three: Knowing the Depths of Christ

The One: Experiencing the Death and Life of Christ

Foreword

I was not a shy teenager, especially when it came to my faith. After I accepted Christ in my early teens, I dropped sports, joined youth group, led a Bible study, and started a Christian rap group ministry. I carried a huge Bible with me everywhere I went (this was decades before the Bible App), and everyone knew what I thought about Jesus.

Except me.

But I didn't realize it at the time. In fact, it wasn't until I got to college that it hit me. In my teen years, I formed my world-view by adopting the beliefs of people around me. I hadn't given much thought to why I believed what I believed. When I started college, some of those ideas got appropriately challenged, which uncovered a gap between my beliefs and my understanding of God. I quickly found my entire belief system unraveling as I began to challenge them one by one.

What remained were ragged remnants of faith I wasn't sure I could trust. I had two choices: I could walk away or I could grow into a new awareness of Christ and what it means to follow Him.

I sought to learn what it means to have faith at the core of my being. I was determined that my foundation would be based on what I grew to understand and what God showed me through His Word.

What I needed was intimacy with Christ. To get there, I had to spend time relentlessly pursuing God. By seeking Him, I gained an understanding I couldn't get from anyone or anywhere else.

Intimacy with Christ wasn't a quick fix that helped me through a rough patch in life. What I learned during that season was that intimacy is essential for me to maintain an ongoing and meaningful relationship with Christ.

I'm not alone in that need. Any of us who follow Jesus are most fulfilled when we have an intimate relationship with Him. And that's where Bob Crosby comes in. Through *The One Jesus Loves*, he guides us toward the richness we can experience when we're not just following Jesus, but following Him closely.

The great news is that it doesn't matter where you are in your relationship. Bob walks us through the different circles of relationships in Jesus' life, ranging from curious and hungry to serving, walking, suffering, celebrating, and sitting with Him. He invites us to recognize each circle as a stage of development and learn how to move further and further in.

Every day, I'm faced with challenges I could never meet on my own strength, and I suspect you might be too. We're dependent on God working through us to accomplish His purposes. Intimacy with Christ is what allows us to have not only faith that He will show up, but joy throughout that journey as we embrace the fullness of walking closely with Him.

Bobby Gruenewald
Founder of YouVersion.com (the Bible App)

1

An Outrageous Request

What do you wish?

—Jesus, Matthew 20:21 nkjv

What is the biggest thing *anyone* ever asked Jesus to do? Do you know? Can you recall?

One day someone approached Jesus and asked him for something no one else had ever had. It was such an extravagant request that everyone who heard stared in disbelief. At that moment and right in broad daylight, with all the disciples looking on, this person walked right up to Jesus, knelt down, and asked him for a ring.

Don't you remember this story?

Perhaps not, but happen it did.

Oh yes, there once was a woman who had the nerve—or should I say boldness—to come to Jesus with a most unique request. It was not for a loaf of bread, a healing, or the answer to a question or a puzzle; it was for a ring.

Yes, a ring.

No, it was not a wedding ring she was after. It was a ring of a different kind. Her question was not "Will you marry me?" but "Will you do something for me, something no one else ever would or even could do?"

A Child's Wish

As a child I was fascinated with the concept of Aladdin's lamp. I cannot count the times I contemplated just what I might ask for if I were lucky enough to be allowed one rub of such a mystery lamp. Maybe it was watching too many episodes of the sitcom *I Dream of Jeannie* when I was a child. Who knows? Anyway, as the story goes, three wishes would be granted—whatever the person desired. You remember the drill.

The more I considered the dreamy notion of a magical lamp as a kid, the more intrigued I became. I imagined in such a situation and with such a golden opportunity, certainly no one could ever wish too big, right? I carefully weighed what I might ask for. The options seemed countless and fascinating:

> "To be king of the world!"
> "To have my own McDonald's!"
> "To become a millionaire!"
> "To be a famous actor."
> "To play quarterback for the NFL!"
> "To own my own jet!"
> "To have a candy store right in my bedroom with an
> unlimited supply!"

And then I realized not one of those wishes was truly the best, not by a long shot. I could do better. The best wish of all suddenly became clear to me. It was so obvious I wondered how

I could have missed it. It was so good it seemed almost too good. I was sure if I could have this wish, I could forgo the other two. With this particular wish, all the others would be unnecessary. That's right. I had whittled it down to only one wish.

And what was the wish?

It was *to have as many more wishes as I wanted for the rest of my life.*

Aha! Bam! There it was. One wish. The gift that keeps on giving or, better said, the wish that keeps on wishing.

"That's not fair," you say. "You weren't playing by the rules! You'd better go back and reread that fairy-tale manual, Crosby! I'm sure there must be a rule against such an open-ended wish. It's right there in the Aladdin's Lamp Constitution and Bylaws, right? Read the fine print."

I beg to differ. After all, as I recall, the three wishes came without stipulation or qualification.

An Opportunity Not to Be Missed

The woman who came to Jesus that day viewed him not as a genie coming out of a lamp but as a King coming into a kingdom. She did not bring with her a list of wishes. She had only one request. But it was really big. Possibly the biggest thing anyone ever asked Jesus for. Most people in that day or even in ours would never presume to ask such a big thing of him. To most, it would sound presumptuous, pompous, and even preposterous.

As a matter of fact, it seemed that in the course of his ministry, Jesus had to remind most of his followers that they could make requests of him. Apparently for much of his ministry, those closest to him did not realize the privileges that being close to him afforded them. On one occasion, Jesus said to his followers: "Until now you have not asked for anything in my name. Ask and you will receive, and your joy will be complete" (John 16:24).

3

The disciples overlooked this great opportunity, but this woman did not. This mom asked big. During the earliest days of Jesus' ministry, she came to him, and she had only one thing to bring. It was not an offering or a sacrifice but a request. Everyone else might have forgotten to ask, but this woman was not about to.

She brought laser-sharp focus and rocket-fueled determination. For some reason, in this woman's mind at least, this one request would be enough. This one thing, this ring of sorts, was important enough for her to risk approaching the man with whom everyone wanted an audience—Jesus, the talk of the town.

The mother of Zebedee's sons came to Jesus with her two boys and, kneeling down, she asked a favor of him.

"What is it you want?" he asked (Matt. 20:20–21).

This was one incredible moment not to be missed. This mother is not mentioned by name. Some traditions, however, hold that she was Salome, who was the sister of Mary, the mother of Jesus. If so, she would have been Jesus' aunt.[1]

Regardless of her actual name, this mom bowed down in tender reverence. The Greek word used here for "kneeling down" is *proskuneo*, which means "to show reverence" or even "to kiss towards."[2] For this moment, this woman entered the most privileged circle, the place of Christ's presence, and brought with her a request for the ring.

The woman who approached Jesus was the mom of James and John, both disciples of Jesus and a part of the Twelve. She wanted something desperately for her sons, and she was determined to go straight to Jesus himself and ask. No passing it through committees for her.

And her request? Or wish? She asked him, "Grant that one of these two sons of mine may sit at your right and the other at your left in your kingdom" (Matt. 20:21).

This mom was on a mission. Her request caught the attention of Jesus, all the disciples, and more than one gospel writer. It was a startling and shocking request because of what it implied and what it sought. The implication was that there are levels of closeness in relationship and proximity to Jesus. Although her sons were already among the twelve disciples of Jesus, she sought for them a place closer still.

Three questions emerge from this story: (1) Are there levels of closeness to Jesus? (2) Can we actually request to sit in those most privileged places? and (3) Can we really ask Jesus for a ring?

I wonder. Don't you?

Well, at least one woman most certainly thought so.

Remember ... followers of Jesus look
for ways to get closer to God.

PART 1

Approaching
Christ, the Man

The Crowds

Observing the Words and Works of Christ

"As I cleared the crest of the hill, I saw something before me I had never seen before. Tens
of thousands of people had so filled the valley
that I couldn't see any land. Pressed together,
they stood on their toes and placed their children on their shoulders hoping to get a peek of
the prophet from Galilee. They said he spoke
with great authority and healed with astounding
power. I was most interested to hear his words
and see his works for myself. But at this distance
and amid so many others, would I even get the
chance?"

2

The Rings of the Lord

Come near to God.

—JAMES 4:8

Jesus had an inner circle. The Bible offers plenty of examples. As a matter of fact, he had several circles or rings of relationship around him.

When the mother of James and John asked Jesus to allow her sons to enter one of those rings, he did not deny her request. However, he did ask them an important question: "Can you drink the cup I am going to drink?" (Matt. 20:22). She did not fully comprehend the magnitude of her request, but Jesus certainly did.

Pastor and author J. Oswald Sanders said, "We are as close to God as we choose to be."[1] God has made it perfectly clear he is vitally interested in being close to every man and woman he has made.

One of my great concerns for the church, however, is that

we not only challenge people to grow closer to Jesus, but that we also find ways to help them know when they are doing just that. After all, what would it be like to meet with an athletic coach week after week for years and hear him say again and again, "Win the game!" but he never lets you play? Or you never find out whether you actually are growing and improving as an athlete? But many Christ followers feel exactly that way. Their leaders and the Bible regularly challenge them to grow, and yet they remain uncertain about whether they actually are growing.

THE RINGS

Consider the rings of relationships that gravitated around Jesus as he walked this planet. I call them the "Rings of the Lord" or the "Circles of Christ." An overview of the Gospels shows there were at least six identifiable groups around Jesus:

1. the Crowds
2. the Five Thousand
3. the Seventy (or some versions translate this as the Seventy-two)
4. the Twelve
5. the Three
6. the One

Each group represents a circle or ring of relationship to the Lord, six stages or areas in relationship to Jesus Christ. They represent places to which people came and experienced him.

Six Rings

Each of the six rings of relationship around Jesus was characterized by something important, even developmental, in our relationship to God. Let's take a quick tour of each:

THE CROWDS. The outermost ring of association with Jesus and the first one we come to is the Crowds. Crowds started to gather around Jesus early in his ministry. These groups at times probably numbered in the tens of thousands and perhaps more. On one occasion, the Pharisees were so astounded by the Crowds they said, "Look, the world has gone after him" (John 12:19 ESV).

Among all the circles of relationship around Jesus, the Crowds were the most impressive in size and yet often the least impressive in soul and substance. The Crowds were the most loosely committed bunch then and still are today. Nonetheless, they represent an important, even precious, place—the place in which all Jesus' followers begin their journey.

The experience of knowing Christ is more of a lifelong journey than a momentary experience. It is related to not just our position on doctrines but our personal choice in pursuing our relationship with Christ and our proximity to him.

The Crowds represent those who follow Jesus to the places of watching and listening. They come to watch what Jesus might do and to hear what he has to say. This place requires the least commitment. It was from this ocean of observers, however, that several fish were eventually caught in Christ's net.

THE FIVE THOUSAND. The Five Thousand did more than observe and evaluate Jesus as he touched and helped them. This group followed him into the desert, desperate not to miss even one of his miraculous works of healing or provision (John 6:1–15).

The Five Thousand represent those who follow Jesus to the places of feeding and healing. They joyfully discovered then, and still do today, that Jesus has many truths to teach and many gifts to offer. Although Jesus willingly and lovingly met so many of their needs and led them to this place, he did not want them to stay there.

THE SEVENTY. Next were the Seventy. Out of the larger groups, a select team rose up to share in Jesus' ministry. You might say these people left the ring of *observation* and entered the ring of *participation*. The Seventy would do the same works they had seen Jesus do.

The Seventy represent those who follow Jesus to the places of working and serving. To this day, many followers of Jesus make it to this ring in their relationship with him but go no farther. Yes, ministry was and is important, but Jesus wanted them to understand that his call was not primarily to *work harder* but to *come closer* to him. That's what this book and this journey are all about.

THE TWELVE. The ring most familiar to us is the Twelve, Jesus' beloved band of brothers, his chosen disciples: "One of those days Jesus went out to a mountainside to pray, and spent the night praying to God. When morning came, he called his disciples to him and chose *twelve* of them, whom he also designated apostles" (Luke 6:12–13, emphasis mine). Christ called this "Shepherd's dozen" to leave all they had and follow him.

The Twelve represent those who walk with Jesus to the places of leaving all and following him. As they entered this ring, they left their own wishes and selfish desires and entered into a new place of surrender to Jesus. But as close to Christ as this ring was, there were closer places still.

THE THREE. One of the innermost circles around Jesus was his cabinet of Three. Church history respectfully dubbed this ring the Triumvirate. *Triumvirate* is a Latin term that refers to a powerful team of three individuals. Of all Jesus' disciples, there were three who saw, heard, and experienced the most.

The Three represent those who follow Jesus to the places of glory and suffering. These were the confidants of Christ. He entrusted them with insights and experiences the rest of the Twelve were apparently unprepared to hear or know.

THE ONE. Ultimately only one person bears the distinction of having been the closest person to Christ during his earthly ministry. I like to think of this person as the One, the closest One.

The One sat right next to Jesus at the Last Supper. The One listened closer to Jesus' words than anyone else and, as a result, recorded more of them than anyone else. The One was the go-to man when Jesus' disciples had a question they wanted to ask him. The One spotted Jesus on the shore when no one else in the boat recognized him. The One followed Christ to at least one place no other among the Twelve would go.

DESIRING GOD

Our desire for God is a gift we must regularly open and engage if we are to fully realize and enjoy it. While salvation is an unconditional gift of God's grace, some intimacies with God come only with a relentless pursuit of him.

Author and pastor A. W. Tozer warned against rigid and overly structured approaches to God and faith: "The whole transaction of religious conversion has been made mechanical and spiritless. . . . We [must remember] that God is a Person and, as such, can be cultivated as any person can."[2]

The promise of Scripture affirms his glorious invitation: "Come near to God and he *will* come near to you" (James 4:8, emphasis mine). Make no mistake, there is one place and one place alone to which Christ wants you to be when it comes to him, and that is *closer.*

Remember . . . followers of Jesus refuse to follow at a distance; if you're not moving closer, you're moving away.

3

Closer

God loves us: not because we are
lovable but because He is love.[1]

—C. S. LEWIS

What is the biggest thing *you* have ever asked God for?

The answer to that question will tell you a lot about yourself and about your faith or the lack thereof. Although God is certainly no genie from an Aladdin's lamp, the Bible tells us "every good and perfect gift is from above, coming down from the Father of the heavenly lights" (James 1:17). It also tells us he is "able to do immeasurably more than all we ask or imagine" (Eph. 3:20).

Dawson Trotman, the late disciple maker who helped Billy Graham train the masses of converts he won to Christ across the world, posed the challenge this way:

Do you know why I often ask Christians, "What's the biggest thing you've asked God for this week?" I remind them that they are going to God, the Father, the Maker of the Universe. The One who holds the world in His hands. What did you ask God for? Did you ask for peanuts, toys, trinkets, or did you ask for continents? I want to tell you, ... people, it's tragic! The little itsy-bitsy things we ask of our Almighty God. Sure, nothing is too small—but also nothing is too big.[2]

What can we find out about the mom who came to Jesus that day asking for the ring, the one who made such a big, bold request, the one who asked for her sons to be allowed to sit at Jesus' left and right? Wouldn't you love to meet this lady?

We don't know a lot about the mother of James and John, her mailing address or her height, but we do know she was a big asker! When it came to asking Jesus, she believed nothing was too big. She wanted to see whether she could get her sons into Jesus' inner circle. If he didn't have one, she was ready for him to start one with her two boys. If her sons wouldn't ask, she would. She was determined to go big or go home!

James and John were already disciples of Jesus. In other words, they had already been called out from among the Crowds and drawn into a closer circle around Jesus, namely, the Twelve. Many would have probably asked this woman, "Don't you think your sons being in the Twelve is already enough?" Nonetheless, their mother felt there *was* something more. Although her sons had already come close to the Master by becoming two of the Twelve, another place was closer still.

She desired more and went after it in a relentless pursuit.

"COME"

Jesus was constantly and winsomely working to bring people ever closer to himself, more deeply into the circles of acquaintance, teaching, and blessing. He was not content, however, for anyone to be merely an acquaintance. He wanted something more. This was his passion. He called people out of the perimeters and toward the inner circles. He was living for it, and he would ultimately die for it.

His words reveal his passion: "Come, follow me . . . and I will make you fishers of men" (Matt. 4:19); "Come to me, all you who are weary and burdened, and I will give you rest" (Matt. 11:28); "Come with me by yourselves to a quiet place and get some rest" (Mark 6:31); and "If anyone is thirsty, let him come to me and drink" (John 7:37).

THE CIRCLES OF CHRIST

Closer to God. This is the soul's deepest quest. Throughout history men and women have tried all sorts of ways to come closer to God. But the glorious quest often can seem elusive and our progress on the journey difficult to measure. Christ followers have embraced a few models throughout the years to assist them in their journey of spiritual growth and formation.

Pastor Kevin DeYoung wrote, "For centuries discipleship instruction (catechesis) has been based on three things: the Apostles' Creed, the Lord's Prayer, and the Ten Commandments. If you wanted the basics of the Christian faith, you learned these three things."[3]

Each of these approaches to spiritual development is a monumental tool for helping us grow in godliness. The Apostles' Creed is a foremost tool of doctrinal development; the Lord's Prayer, an aid to our meditation on God and our petitions to him; and the Ten Commandments, a guide to our moral and character development. A biblical model a bit more relational in its design, however, would be helpful. This book proposes such a model with these thoughts:

The Apostles' Creed helps us with *right beliefs*.
The Lord's Prayer assists us with *focused intercessions*.
The Ten Commandments define *clear morals* in the eyes of God.
The Circles of Christ might help display *more vivid intimacies* with God.

Whereas the other models focus us as Christ followers on doctrine, prayer, and morality, the Circles of Christ *focus on proximity and place*, that is, on our closeness and connectedness to Christ. Instead of majoring on right information, the approach of this book takes us to *places of transformation*, to *brighter views and viewpoints of Jesus*. It is a journey of walking with those who first walked the closest to Christ.

These six spheres of spiritual formation, the Circles of Christ, are not stages that determine our merit or value; rather, they are areas of experience in our intimacy with Jesus. And they do not necessarily function in a linear fashion. They represent areas of intimacy with God that we enter, visit, and revisit and that help to form and conform us to the image of Christ (Rom. 8:29).

God unconditionally gives his grace to us. We cannot earn it. But while grace is freely given, we are called to pursue relentlessly our experience of intimacy with God. This truth is evident from the Old Testament to the New. In Jeremiah, God said, "You will seek me and find me when you seek me with all your heart" (29:13), and in James we are told, "Come near to God and he will come near to you" (4:8).

Jesus came to reveal the God who is not a lofty leader

isolated in his transcendence but a passionate Father longing to bring his sons and daughters closer. What about you? Have you felt close to God today, recently, or ever? And just what makes you feel close to him?

The Bible shows Jesus to be more than a messenger of doctrine. Instead, the Gospels give us a broad tapestry of people's experiences *with* him and their encounters *of* him. Resounding within each of the four accounts of his life and ministry, from Matthew to John, is an appeal reverberating with this message: Get to know him! Come closer!

How Close?

But just how close can a person come to Christ today? And what does it take to cultivate the kind of closeness that quenches the God-thirst within your soul and mine? What were the secret insights and experiences shared by the people who were the closest to Jesus during his earthly life and ministry? These questions have drawn me to write this book. Thank you for joining me on this journey of discovery.

Jesus' call was toward a deeper and more intimate walk and relationship with him. While God's grace provides and offers us the relationship, intimacy allows us to fully enjoy and experience it. Make no mistake, grace is an unconditional gift, but intimacy with Jesus is *a relentless pursuit.*

Remember... followers want to
be only one place—closer.

4

Jesus' POV

When he saw the crowds ...

—MATTHEW 9:36

If you want to get the attention of a roomful of teenagers, turn something wild loose. A little touch of chaos in the atmosphere periodically is an asset to any youth group.

Years ago when I was a youth pastor, I turned something loose as I got ready to tell the parable of the lost sheep (Luke 15:1–7). After a little searching, I found a modern-day shepherdess, a middle-aged woman, on the outskirts of our town, Rochester, New York. My wife and I went out to visit the shepherdess on her farm, and she agreed to come to the city and talk about what she had come to understand about the nature of sheep and how she tended them.

Just as I started to speak at the youth meeting that Wednesday night, the back door swung open and in ran a little lamb. That cute animal cut back and forth through the rows and legs of students. The place went wild with excitement. Inserting a live animal into the environment brought a livelier view to the Bible story I wanted to tell.

Jesus has a POV altogether different from ours. POV is a literary and theatrical term used to describe "point of view." POV is the viewpoint, angle, or perspective through which someone observes settings, situations, or people. But what was Jesus' POV? The gospel of Matthew tells us the way he viewed the Crowds: "When [Jesus] saw the crowds, he had compassion on them, because they were harassed and helpless, like sheep without a shepherd" (Matt. 9:36).

The word *crowd* is used more than one hundred times in the Gospels. Crowds frequently surrounded Jesus. Floyd McClung, the international director of All Nations, a church planting and leadership training network, wrote:

> [Jesus] was just as intentional about reaching the crowds as He was individuals, but with distinctly different approaches.
>
> . . . Jesus saw interaction with the crowds as a way of planting seeds in people's hearts (Luke 8:4–18), a way of arousing spiritual interest, and a way of finding disciples to be taught. He was looking for those who were hungry for more, so He could invest His time wisely with them.[1]

Looking at the Crowds, Jesus saw that the challenges people faced varied. Even now, he sees that you and I, and also the Crowds among which we find ourselves, struggle with the fact that we have

- an enemy (thus, we're "harassed");
- a hopelessness (thus, we're "helpless"); and

- a lonely lostness (thus, we're "like sheep without a shepherd").

I hope you know just how much Jesus loves you. One way to find out is to know just how he *sees* you.

CHARACTERISTICS OF SHEEP

Sheep generally run in flocks, in groups. This is where Christ often finds us first, among the Crowds. Remember, *the Crowds represent those who follow Jesus to the places of watching and listening.* The Crowds often surrounded Jesus. This experience for Jesus never smacked of a celebrity with his fans; rather he was a Shepherd with his sheep.

The shepherdess who visited our youth group gave us insights into sheep and their behavior. Hearing these was an eye-opener for me. Let's just say, I could identify. Christ also sees these tendencies within you and me.

Sheep Have No Real Sense of Direction

We know from the Gospels that Christ came to earth "to seek and to save the lost" (Luke 19:10). Sheep have a propensity for getting lost.

Knowing Christ and growing closer to him begins with a sense of need. For the earliest followers of Jesus who heard about him and made their way into the Crowds, their focal point at this place was their questions. But because of the vast multitudes, they did not have the opportunity to ask Jesus. We can only imagine the questions they must have asked themselves:

- *Is Jesus really someone come from God?*
- *Can he really help me with my struggle?*
- *Does he understand how I feel?*

- *Is there some way I can get closer to him in order to gain his help?*

Sheep Are Quite Helpless Against Predators

Christ told us, "The thief [Satan] comes only to steal and kill and destroy" (John 10:10). When you sense an enemy trying to diminish or harm you, Jesus sees your need and can rescue and protect you.

Sheep Left Alone Will Actually Eat Themselves into a Lost Place

Even in the Old Testament, Isaiah said, "We all, like sheep, have gone astray" (53:6). Our default mode tends to find us wandering to places that hurt more than help us.

Sheep Are Weak

And often, so are we. Yet the apostle Paul took time in 2 Corinthians to talk about our weaknesses and how even they can make a place for Christ's strength to be revealed (check out 2 Corinthians 12 for *strong* points on weakness).

Sheep Get Dirty Easily

Everything seems to stick to their wool, and sheep do not clean or groom themselves. Our lives and souls can get quickly and easily soiled in today's world. We often struggle to find a lasting sense of holiness and wholeness on our own. We really do need a shepherd to clean us up.

Sheep Are Gregarious, Social Creatures That Do Better in Numbers

We all do better in community than we do alone. We are created for community. We are formed for friendship. Isolation and loneliness tend to wither our souls; community helps grow them.

Sheep Require More Care than Any Other Livestock

They are time-intensive animals to raise, and they require much from their caretakers. So do we. Just ask your pastor (shepherd) or your parent.

Sheep Are Timid and Easily Panicked

They stampede easily and are prey to mob reactions. Is it any wonder Jesus so often said to his followers, "Fear not"?

PATHOS

The Bible's statement that Jesus was "moved with compassion" is a deep expression of soul, one full of pathos, passion, and heart. According to *The Message*, "His heart broke."

Since we are "harassed" by an enemy, Jesus alone can overcome Satan's power in our lives.

Since we are "helpless," Christ alone is our "ever-present help in trouble" (Ps. 46:1).

Since we are "like sheep without a shepherd," Jesus alone is the Shepherd who "lays down his life for the sheep" (John 10:11).

Jesus sees the challenges, struggles, hurts, and pains of our sheepness and sheepishness. One reason God sent his Son to earth was to make sure we would know just how he, God the Father, feels about us and just how he sees us. He is moved by the needs of your life. He sees *you* that way. No matter what challenge you face, you are not alone. When it comes to you and me, Jesus has a unique POV. He sees Crowds in a unique way, like "sheep without a shepherd." And isn't that the only way a Good Shepherd ever would?

Remember . . . in the Crowds, we discover
how much we need a Shepherd.

5

The Bigger Story

The kingdom of God is within you.

—LUKE 17:21

Crowds are compelling. That truth was underlined for me at a Red Sox game I attended with my wife when I lived in Boston. For one unforgettable moment I was overcome with the sense of the Crowds.

Leaving Fenway Park that night when we made our way back to the car, I saw a scene I won't soon forget. In front of me was a river of thousands and thousands of people streaming down the road mostly clad in their color-coordinated Red Sox attire and paraphernalia. I said to my wife, Pam, "Now *that's* a crowd of biblical proportions."

What really hit me was the sense that all of us as humans have an incredible need to be a part of Crowds, of bigger groups, of something bigger than ourselves, of a bigger story. That night in

Boston, those fans were not just individuals; they were a part of Red Sox Nation, a term popularly used among the Boston faithful.

Being a part of the Crowds is so compelling in sports that people are willing to sacrifice something of themselves to be a part of something bigger. It becomes such a connection that we almost forget about our own names and identities, and we find pleasure, instead, in wearing the same names on our heads (caps) and shirts (jerseys). We get lost together in a bigger story.

The earliest buzz on the streets of ancient Palestine about Jesus must have gone something like this:

"Have you heard about this man Jesus?"

"Apparently he has been speaking of some kind of new kingdom he plans to bring."

"What a storyteller. Fascinating stuff!"

The Crowds around Jesus were growing. He wasn't just the talk of the town; he was the talk of the nation. Matthew recalled those earliest moments:

> "He went throughout all Galilee, teaching in their synagogues and proclaiming the gospel of the kingdom and healing every disease and every affliction among the people. *So his fame spread* throughout all Syria, and they brought him all the sick, those afflicted with various diseases and pains, those oppressed by demons, epileptics, and paralytics, and he healed them. And *great crowds followed him.*" (Matt. 4:23–25 ESV, emphasis mine)

As Jesus traveled, taught, and healed, we are told that "his fame" spread throughout all Syria. The result of that fame spreading was, you guessed it, Crowds, and Jesus was drawing "great" Crowds. Jesus' ministry was permeating popular culture; it was creating a buzz in the world around him![1]

Even though much of the excitement about Jesus must have

been the miracles he was working, notice that what Matthew cited first among the list of Jesus' works were his "teaching" and "proclaiming." Jesus' role was as proclaimer at that stage in the development of the onlookers. He was frequently teaching and telling people about God, his ways, and his kingdom.

When we enter the Crowds in our own spiritual growth, our motivation is our curiosity; we are drawn to Jesus' teachings. Often we are first introduced to Jesus, his teachings, and his works while in the Crowds.

My Journey into the Crowds

I remember a particular television event in my home when I was seven or eight years old. It was the airing of a Billy Graham Evangelistic Crusade. Whenever Billy preached the gospel on television, my parents always watched. Usually it was only once or twice a year for a three- or four-night sequence.

There was something about the presence in our home during those nights when Billy preached. Everything quieted down. My parents, who had a nominal Christian background then, had my younger brother and me sit with them and doodle or draw as we watched the hourlong services that always included a special song or two by a Christian musician (even Johnny Cash at times), a choir number, maybe the testimony of a well-known believer, and a fiery sermon from Graham.

No, I didn't make my commitment to Christ at a Graham event, but I am convinced that the repeated exposure to those messages helped form the commitment I made later. I could feel the tug of the Holy Spirit as people poured from the stadium seats and crowds to the sports fields to yield their lives to Christ. Thank God for Billy Graham and his compassion on the Crowds. God only knows how many souls among those technological Crowds he influenced, including mine.

THE KINGDOM CALL

The kingdom Jesus proclaimed was the circle into which God was calling people. Jesus spoke to people within their current smaller circles and stories and called them into the bigger one, the biggest one—the kingdom of God, the Grand Narrative. Dallas Willard, late professor of philosophy and a minister, said it so well: "[Jesus] made 'disciples' by presenting them with the kingdom and introducing them into it by reaching their hearts, changing their vision of reality and their intentions for life."[2]

In our own journey of following Christ, the Crowds represent *those who have come to a place of watching and listening to Christ.* What about you? Have you come yet to this place of the Crowds in your walk with Christ? Do you find yourself there now? Are you *watching*? Are you *listening*?

Jesus is calling us out of our smaller stories and into the Bigger Story of the kingdom of God. He is calling us out of the pettiness of our selfish pursuits and into the broadened panorama of his divine plan. Can't you hear him endeavoring to stretch your view?

"Seek first the kingdom of God and his righteousness" (Matt. 6:33 ESV).
"The kingdom of God has come near to you" (Luke 10:9).
"The kingdom of God is within you" (Luke 17:21 ESV).

When Jesus says, "Seek first the kingdom of God," the word *first* in the original language does not mean first on a long list of things to do. Rather, he is speaking about priority. He is telling his followers to focus on their Father's kingdom and his righteous ways, and then everything else will take care of itself.[3]

When I go to a Red Sox game or any game for that matter, I watch and listen. I watch the players on the field playing the game and hope my team will win; I listen to the commentary of the announcer and pay attention to what he says about the game. But here's the deal: although I am at the game, I am not actually playing in it. I'm not a participant; I'm only a spectator.

We first see Christ from the vantage point of Crowds, but he calls us to move beyond Crowds to a closer place. Yes, we can observe him and his Bigger Story from our stadium seats, and that is a great place to start; in many instances, it may be the only one. But as it turns out, Christ did not come seeking an audience or fans; he came seeking souls and lives that would follow him fully. Jesus beckons us into his Bigger Story.

Remember... in the Crowds, we follow Christ to the places of watching and listening.

6

The Day Jesus Followed

Jesus rose and followed him.

—MATTHEW 9:19 ESV

Praying in my home study in Ohio that day, I was wondering what door God would open next for my life. My wife and I were at a place where we felt a season of change coming in our lives and work. I had been praying about the Boston area and sensing a call to plant or lead a church there. It was a time of searching and uncertainty.

A brochure with a picture of the Boston skyline on it lay on my desk. My seven-year-old daughter, Kristin, wandered into my office. She noticed the brochure, pointed to it, and asked, "Where is this, Daddy?"

I replied, "Oh, sweetheart. That is a city called Boston. It is in Massachusetts. Mom and I are praying about this city."

"Hmmm. Do you know what I think, Daddy?" she asked, admiring the picture.

"No, Kristin. What's that?"

"I think you are going to move there and be a pastor there, and they are going to have a school for me to go to there."

I sat up straight in my chair. It wasn't just what she said, but the matter-of-fact certainty with which she said it, as if it were already a done deal.

Kristin's comments stunned me. At that time, unbeknownst to her, we were pondering what a move to Boston might look like. When I told Pam what Kristin said, she, too, was stunned and intrigued.

There was a particular day in Jesus' life and ministry when he must have felt much the same way. Someone said something he found instantly and absolutely compelling. In the story, a father showed up while Jesus was addressing a crowd of John the Baptist's disciples:

> While [Jesus] was saying these things to [John's disciples], behold, a ruler came in and knelt before him, saying, "My daughter has just died, but come and lay your hand on her, and she will live." And Jesus rose and followed him, with his disciples. . . . And when Jesus came to the ruler's house and saw the flute players and the crowd making a commotion, he said, "Go away, for the girl is not dead but sleeping." And they laughed at him. But when the crowd had been put outside, he went in and took her by the hand, and the girl arose. And the report of this went through all that district. (Matt. 9:18–19, 23–26 esv)

Jesus Hears

This was a day when we might say Jesus followed someone else's faith. While Jesus responded to a question from the disciples of

John on a controversial theological subject, "a ruler came in and knelt before him" (v. 18).

Just picture it. Amid the Crowds surrounding Jesus, one man—a ruler at that, most likely a local official—had the audacity to walk right in and kneel before Jesus. He came uninvited, yet quite undeterred. He came with worship but also with something to say.

Here are the three things he said:

1. "My daughter has just died." (Is it any wonder why this man came to Jesus without being invited? Imagine this dad's desperation.)
2. "Come and lay your hand on her" (seven words of clear and certain pleading).
3. "And she will live" (four miraculous words).

This father whose daughter had just died came to Jesus not full of grief or despair but full of faith. He laid it all out, and Jesus responded without hesitation. And this father brought three gifts for Jesus. First, he brought his *pain* as he said, "My daughter has just died." Next, he brought his *plea* as he requested Jesus do something about it, that he "come and lay [his] hand on her." Third, he brought his *profession of faith* to Jesus when he asserted that "she will live." These three focused offerings immediately tapped the compassion of Christ for this one who suddenly emerged from the Crowds.

Here's something else, something truly amazing. In response to this father's immediate prayer, we have no record of Jesus actually saying anything. On the contrary, it appears he said nothing at all, but he immediately did something: he "rose." The prayer brought Jesus right to his feet: "Jesus rose and followed him, with his disciples" (v. 19).

It is encouraging to know your faith can invite Jesus not only into your heart but also into your home. It seems faith not only follows Christ; in a sense, it is followed by Christ. Since "without faith it is impossible to please God" (Heb. 11:6), it is quite clear just how pleased Jesus was with it. In this case, it literally moved him.

"Go Away"

Once Jesus arrived at the ruler's house, the first thing he saw was not a daughter's dead body but Crowds gathered in and around the house "making a commotion" (Matt. 9:23 ESV). They were apparently engaged in a rather raucous mourning ritual. But the atmosphere they created was not the one Christ desired. Before healing would come, the commotion had to cease. Jesus' words to the crowd were not "come unto me," but "go away." On this occasion, he wasn't drawn to the Crowds; he was repelled by them. He told them, "Go away, for the girl is not dead but sleeping" (v. 24).

The response of the Crowds was not to echo Jesus' faith or follow it. No amens were heard in this bunch. They did something else; they "laughed at [Jesus]" (v. 24). Can I just say I wouldn't recommend doing that? They thought his statement of faith was preposterous. Then something was done that precipitated the fulfillment of the miracle at hand. It appears that the ruler of the house, the father, or perhaps Jesus' disciples had to drive the Crowds and the commotion of doubt right out of the house. To let something in that Jesus wanted, some people had to be sent out.

In the stage of our spiritual development in which we find ourselves among the Crowds, listening to Jesus becomes the important next step. In a sense, our faith experience at this level is developing a *hearing* faith. Apparently Jesus wanted to whittle this group down to people of faith.

Before we see the fulfillment of the miracle here, the Crowds had to be "put outside" (v. 25). The moment they were gone, the atmosphere cleared for faith, and just look at what happened then: Jesus "went in and took her by the hand, and the girl arose" (v. 25). Once the Crowds were removed and the commotion cleared from the house, faith had a chance to grow and healing came. In Luke's retelling of this story he added that "her parents were astonished" (8:56). Mark wrote, "They were immediately overcome with amazement" (5:42 ESV).

Our daughter Kristin's statement of faith in my home study that day was certain and clear. Its simplicity and sincerity cleared some of the commotion and worry from my mind. Although her words did not determine our coming steps, they certainly helped to confirm them. In a sense, that day Kristin's certainty and faith made me want to follow. Faith has that effect on the soul. Within a few short months, we were pastoring a church in the Boston area and continued there almost fifteen years. And, oh yes, by the way, that church had a school Kristin attended along with her siblings, just the way she had said.

Remember . . . in the Crowds, the commotion in our lives has to be cleared so we can hear the words of Jesus.

7

Crowdsurfing: Z's Story

He was seeking to see who Jesus was.

—LUKE 19:3 ESV

One of the toughest crowds to navigate well would certainly have to be the U.S. Congress. Political pundits and lobbyists, nonetheless, do it all the time in Washington, DC. At least one man I know, however, decided to take on that challenge for another reason altogether. He did it for Jesus' sake. His name is Dick Foth.

Dick has been a pastor, writer, leader, and university president for many years. He is a fascinating communicator and Bible teacher and as engaging a conversationalist as you'll ever meet. All these gifts have served him well as he has walked the corridors of Congress and befriended so many leaders there.

A few years ago I heard Dick describe a fresh way he had found of telling the gospel of Jesus one-on-one. Dick said that by coming to this earth, Jesus was telling every person in the world these four things:

1. "I'm going to leave *my* place."
2. "I'm going to come to *your* place."
3. "I'm going to *take* your place."
4. "Then, we're going back to *my* place."

What a personal, clear, and compelling way to describe the gospel! These four movements of Christ paint a vivid picture.

One of the most famous stories of Crowds, interestingly enough, is about an individual named Zacchaeus. In this chapter, let's just call him Z to keep it simple. Here's his story:

> [Jesus] entered Jericho and was passing through. And behold, there was a man named Zacchaeus. He was a chief tax collector and was rich. And he was seeking to see who Jesus was, but on account of the crowd he could not, because he was small in stature. So he ran on ahead and climbed up into a sycamore tree to see him, for he was about to pass that way. And when Jesus came to the place, he looked up and said to him, "Zacchaeus, hurry and come down, for I must stay at your house today." So he hurried and came down and received him joyfully. And when they saw it, they all grumbled, "He has gone in to be the guest of a man who is a sinner." And Zacchaeus stood and said to the Lord, "Behold, Lord, the half of my goods I give to the poor. And if I have defrauded anyone of anything, I restore it fourfold." And Jesus said to him, "Today salvation has come to this house, since he also is a son of Abraham. For the Son of Man came to seek and to save the lost." (Luke 19:1–10 ESV)

Z "was seeking to see who Jesus was" (v. 3). He wanted to know more. He was determined to investigate on his own, to get out of his house or his comfort zone, and to hit the street in search of this man. But he soon met some challenges.

Z's Challenges: The Things Going on Around Him

The challenges Z faced in finding out just "who Jesus was" are not all that different from those we face today. Consider this:

Z wanted to see Jesus, but he had a physical limitation: "he was small in stature" (v. 3). Put simply, Z was short. He was a little dude.

Z had a title and the power that went along with it: "he was a chief tax collector" (v. 2), and Z's position and role in his town would have separated him from the common people. He was the IRS director of his day. As Kent Ingle, a Christian university president, said, "He might have been a 'wee little man,' but in Jericho he was a Big Shot!"[1] Yet the people did not trust Z in his role. One commentator explained it this way: "As chief tax collector Zacchaeus was head of a tax-farming corporation with collectors who extorted the people, then paid him before he paid the Romans. He was the kingpin of the Jericho tax cartel and had the scruples of a modern-day crack dealer. . . . Not a likely candidate for the kingdom!"[2]

Z was financially secure: he "was rich" (v. 2). Z no doubt dealt with some resentment from townspeople, envious of his wealth and suspicious of his practices.

Z had been labeled by the religious people in his community as "a man who is a sinner" (v. 7). It seems the Crowds had already sized him up and were convinced he was irredeemable.

Z found that Crowds were coming between him and Jesus. Sometimes the size of the Crowds, as well as the pressure of popular ideas and opinions (for example, pop culture) can crowd out our view of Jesus. Some of the obstacles between Z and Jesus were cultural.

Some things to remember about Crowds:

Crowds can be fun.
Crowds can be magnetic.
Crowds are drawn to what is currently popular.
Crowds are exciting.
Crowds can be confusing.
Crowds can be intimidating.
Crowds can change quickly.

While you may learn more about Christ while among the Crowds, beware of staying there too long. The main temptation of just staying in the Crowds is to casually watch Christ from a distance and never really see; to partially listen to his Word and never really hear.

WHAT WE CAN LEARN FROM Z

At the beginning of Z's faith journey, he had likely heard some of the buzz about Jesus. As a result he became curious. This is how we often begin to find Christ. We become curious, intrigued, interested. But Z was just getting started. His questions likely included these:

- "Who is this man Jesus?"
- "I have all the money I need, but something central to my life is still empty. Might he hold the answer?"
- "Is there a way to get through the Crowds and closer to Jesus?"

Z was passionate to see more, but the Crowds came between him and Jesus. He could have tried to go around or get ahead of the people. Instead Z had to find a way to rise above the Crowds.

A CLEARER VIEW

Somehow, some way, God by his Spirit wants to help us rise above the Crowds, above the opinions, above the noise, and to see Jesus and to be seen by him. For Z, a sycamore tree provided the necessary lift. What will lift you above the Crowds and help you see Jesus?

Did you notice what Jesus did once he spotted Z? He actually invited himself over to Z's house. Jesus didn't wait for an invitation, and he seldom does. "When Jesus came to the place, he looked up and said to him, 'Zacchaeus, hurry and come down, for I must stay at your house today '" (v. 5). How do you like that?—Jesus invites himself over to Z's house. In his own way that day, Jesus told Zacchaeus:

"I'm going to leave my place in heaven."
"I'm going to come to your place in Jericho, your house, in fact!"
"I'm going to take your place on a cross."
"Then, we're going back to my place in heaven."

When we are in the circle of the Crowds, watching and listening to Jesus are the focus. But there is yet a place in which we can come closer to Christ. At this next place we move from hearing and seeing his works to experiencing them.

While Dick found a way to surf the Washington Crowds in order to *introduce* Christ, Zacchaeus surfed the Crowds in

Jericho in order to *meet* him. And once he did, Jesus said, "What's for dinner, Z? I'm coming over to your place!"

Remember . . . in the Crowds, we have to overcome the obstructions around us so we can get a clearer view of Jesus.

The Five Thousand

Enjoying the Gifts and Graces of Christ

"As soon as I heard that the man from Galilee was heading to the wilderness, I got myself ready for a day trip and hurried out with dozens of others from my village to see him. Maybe this time the crowds would not be as large as before. Perhaps I could get close enough to see Jesus' expressions as he talked more about God. Instead of hearing others who stood closer describe the healings, perhaps I may even see one this time. Or at best, maybe I will stand close enough for him to see me and to recognize my need that has become so obvious to me as, I'm sure, it is to others."

8

The Day Jesus Wanted to Be Alone

He withdrew . . . to a desolate place by himself.

—MATTHEW 14:13 ESV

When I pulled up to our house after work that day with my wife, Pamela, I could not believe what I saw. There must have been ten cars parked in front of our house, including the car our eighteen-year-old son drove. My blood heated up instantly.

"Pam, can you believe it?" I said as we walked toward the front door. "That boy must have brought a dozen of his friends to our house without asking us!" Already I knew the lecture I would give Rob as soon as his friends left.

When I threw the front door open, I was startled at what I saw: a group of teenagers standing in our foyer, holding hands,

49

and praying. I froze for a moment. Not what I was expecting. Not at all.

There was a day when Jesus also wanted just to be alone. The day he fed the Five Thousand did not start off with any fanfare; rather, it began with distressing news. John the Baptist, Jesus' cousin, had just been executed. He literally lost his head to Herod, the ruler of Galilee.

The text reveals Jesus' humanness. When he got the news, the last place he wanted to be was in the Crowds. Instead, "he withdrew from there in a boat to a desolate place by himself" (Matt. 14:13 ESV). And would anyone question why?

Jesus was hit with an emotional grenade. With the news of a dearly beloved relative and the front man to his mission brutally murdered, Jesus just wanted to be alone. You know the feeling. He needed time to let it sink in, time to grieve, time to reflect, and time to pray. He "withdrew," he pulled away from his normal duties, from his followers, and perhaps most of all from the Crowds in order to be alone with God and his new realities.

TIME TO MYSELF?

But the Crowds would have nothing of the sort. Although this was arguably one of the most stressful days in Christ's earthly life, the people would not allow him to be "by himself" for long. In fact, "when the crowds heard [that Jesus had withdrawn himself], they followed him on foot from the towns" (Matt. 14:13 ESV).

I don't know about you, but in the same situation I would have probably said, "Enough is enough. I need some time to myself. The Crowds will just have to wait."

Not Jesus. Nowhere close. Jesus had a much different

reaction. When he saw the "great crowd," instead "he had compassion on them and healed their sick" (v. 14 ESV). Somehow he set aside his human pain and grieving and changed emotional gears, prioritizing the needs of the people coming to him for help. Instead of expecting the Crowds to understand his struggle, Jesus focused the spotlight on theirs. That's compassion.

When it comes to our walk with Christ, the Five Thousand represent those who *follow Jesus to the places of healing and feeding*. Many did so then; many still do so today. This journey brought this bunch to a new place in their faith experience. Now they would experience more than listening to Jesus; *they would experience him* in his power and provision. As the Crowds set out to find him, surely they hoped this time it would be not quite so crowded as usual.

My Journey into the Five Thousand

God used a group of Christian teenagers from Mooresville, North Carolina, to lead me to Christ the week I turned sixteen. My family and I had set up camp in Myrtle Beach the night before we first met them. Out of two thousand campsites at this park, this group of about twenty youth just so happened to set up camp right next door to us. Long story short, within a few days, these teenagers had shared their faith with me and shown me a clear picture of what following Christ would look like in a teenager's life. My life was forever changed.

But my Five Thousand experience came a few months later. The year before my conversion, I had picked up pneumonia and was out of school for quite some time. Then a few months after coming to Christ in Myrtle Beach, I got sick again with the same symptoms, a repeat of the previous year. This time, however, I remember going into the bathroom at Keenan High School in Columbia, South Carolina, overcome with the symptoms. The mirror showed me how bad I looked. Deep within me I sensed God saying, *I can heal you right now.*

Usually I would have gone to the nurse's office and gotten a pass to go home. I felt encouraged in that moment to pray a bold prayer. So, I prayed something like this: "Jesus, would you touch and heal me right now? Please, Lord." Amazingly within a few moments, I started to feel better, stronger, and refreshed. I went back to class and took my seat and had no further symptoms. As small as that may seem to some, I must say it was huge to me and my faith journey. I felt God's healing touch for the first time.

"What Do You Want Me to Do for You?"

The Five Thousand represent those who come to Christ drawn by the sense of his ministry, his provision, and even his miracles. He is seen at this place as the Christ we need to help us through our struggles, hungers, and human needs. At this place in our growth we are desperate to discover him as our Provider.

A time would come in the lives of some of Jesus' followers in which he would call upon them to care about and share in his struggles, but not so on this day or with this group. When he saw the Five Thousand, he seemed to put on his Physician's uniform; he "healed their sick" (Matt. 14:14). He put their interests before his own. At this place the follower can sense Christ asking, "What do you want me to do for you?" (Mark 10:51).

When I flung open our front door that afternoon, my son and his prayer circle were abruptly interrupted.

"Oh, hi, Dad," Rob said. "My friends and I are here to pray for Justin." He pointed to his friend standing by his side and said, "You remember, Dad. Justin goes to school with me. His dad passed away from cancer a couple of days ago. I asked some friends to come over so we could pray for him together. I hope that's all right."

"Oh, sure, son," I said. "Of course that's fine."

My frustration quickly turned to embarrassment. The crowd of teenagers in my house suddenly turned into sheep without a shepherd. The people in the room were the same people I had just seen, but my view of them was instantly transformed.

When Jesus saw the Crowds, he was thinking about them and their needs. When I first saw the crowd of cars, I was thinking about something else.

Myself.

Remember . . . in the Five Thousand, we follow Christ to the places of feeding and healing.

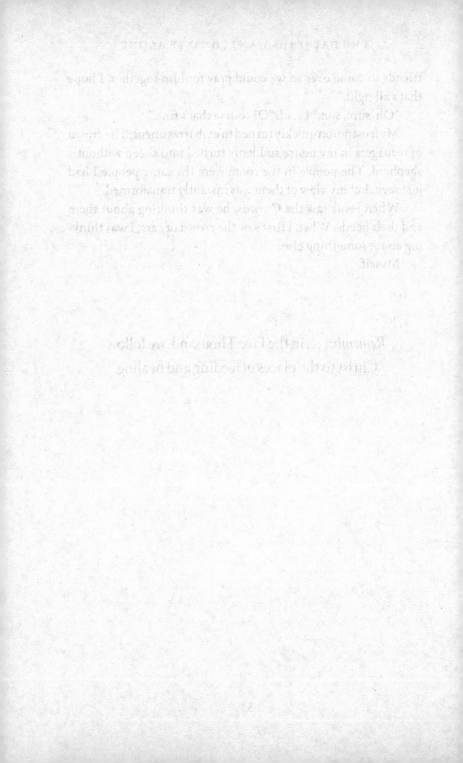

9

Sack Lunch Spirituality

What is that in your hand?

—Exodus 4:2

Amid a windfall of miracles and supernatural events among the
Five Thousand, Jesus' disciples seemed worried. While blinded
eyes opened, lame legs walked, and deaf ears heard, the Twelve
were concerned about another need: getting hungry.

> Philip answered . . . , "It would take more than half a year's
> wages to buy enough bread for each one to have a bite!"
>
> Another of his disciples, Andrew, Simon Peter's brother,
> spoke up, "Here is a boy with five small barley loaves and two
> small fish, but how far will they go among so many?"
>
> Jesus said, "Have the people sit down." There was plenty
> of grass in that place, and they sat down (about five thousand
> men were there). Jesus then took the loaves, gave thanks, and

distributed to those who were seated as much as they wanted.
He did the same with the fish. (John 6:7–11)

The boy with the sack lunch during the feeding of the Five
Thousand learned a secret almost everyone else in the group
most certainly missed. The secret of surrender. The moment
this boy extended his hand and offered his lunch to Jesus, he
took a step out of his own agenda and a step into Christ's; his
focus went from his selfish interests to kingdom work. While
it appeared that he was giving something he needed most in
that hour—namely, food—he was just about to gain something
much greater.

Here they were: the Five Thousand, freshly touched by
God's presence. Each one of them who had been sick was now
healed. At that moment, they must have been the healthiest pack
of people in Palestine.

But there was one problem: now they were really hungry.
And to make matters worse, they were way out in the wilderness. The nearest food markets were days away.

Imagine you were in that desperate place, feeling healthy
but hungry. And you have something no one else in the Five
Thousand has—lunch. Somehow among all the mothers in
Palestine, yours had the foresight to prepare a sack lunch for
you. What would you do?

I know what I would have done. I would have probably
slipped off to a private spot long enough to enjoy it. Or, at the
most, shared it with my immediate family, making sure I had a
bigger piece than did any of my siblings. Not this lad. He caught
something before Jesus ever taught it, with words, that is. He
learned the secret of surrender.

This young man, like all the rest of the Five Thousand,
had received from God. Maybe he was healed, as many of the
rest of them were. As a matter of fact, I think that may be what

motivated him to give his lunch to Jesus. It is doubtful that when he placed it in Jesus' hands, he had any idea of what the Lord intended to do. For all he knew, he was offering Jesus one meal for himself. The Lord had ministered to (and probably healed) him. Now the least he could do was minister to (or serve) Jesus in some way.

That young man had the same thing you have to offer—what God has already given you, what he has placed in your hands—that and nothing more.

John's telling of this story adds a bit to it. It shows that the challenge of feeding the Five Thousand was a big problem: "One of [Jesus'] disciples, Andrew, Simon Peter's brother, said to him, 'There is a boy here who has five barley loaves and two fish, but *what are they for so many?*'" (6:8–9 ESV, emphasis mine).

WHAT'S IN YOUR HANDS?

When Moses in the Old Testament was at a loss over how he was going to serve God, God asked him a question: "What is that in your hand?" (Ex. 4:2). And what was in his hand was a staff, a simple walking stick. I am sure there was nothing especially appealing to the eye about that staff of Moses'. After all it was just a stick.

What is most amazing about that stick, however, is not what it accomplished in Moses' hands, but what it accomplished in Moses' hands after he had placed it in God's hands. Before he placed it in God's hands, he had used it through countless journeys in the desert, to prod off predators, to clear the path, and to steady his steps on rugged terrain. After Moses took his hands off it and gave it to God, it was used to lead Moses off his path and back onto God's, to fight and devour the serpents of sorcerers, to lead God's people out of bondage, to part and pave a pathway through an ocean, and to draw water out of a rock.

As Moses' stick, it was ordinary; as the rod of God, it was truly extraordinary.

It is interesting to me the Lord chose to use that young lad's lunch. We know from reading the Bible that God can make something out of nothing. He made the heavens and the earth by the power of his words. Whipping up a banquet for this bunch seems like child's play compared to that. However, he chose not to make it out of nothing or even to speak it into existence. No, he wanted to take what was in this young man's hands and bless it, even multiply it.

What about you? What do you have in your hands? What has God given you to use for his glory? Give it back to him. Present it to him intentionally. Place it in his hands even now and you will no longer just have a possession. You will have a ministry.

You may say, "But I don't think I have anything that can be used for a ministry."

Are you sure? Consider this:

Do you have a house? God wants to make it a place of ministry by filling it with people in need of hospitality.

Do you have a spouse? God wants to make you a powerful partnership of prayer.

Do you have children? God wants to use you to shape them into men and women of God.

Do you have an income? God wants you to honor him and to strengthen other ministries with the "firstfruits" of it (Ex. 23:19).

Do you have a voice? God wants to season your words with grace to touch other lives.

Do you have feet? God wants to lead you to places where you can share his love with others.

Do you have hands? God wants to touch lives, to embrace the lonely and serve needs through those hands.

Do you have a talent? God wants to bless people with it.

Do you have a skill? God wants to enrich lives and his church with it.

Do you have a sack lunch? God wants you to share it and see how it multiplies.

What you have in your hands is what God has given you to show others what you have in your heart—the love of God. When we use our time, talents, gifts, skills, and interests to serve others, God has a way of multiplying the impact and influence of these things many times over. And when we use them they draw us farther out of the Crowds and alongside Jesus to serve the Crowds and individuals yet waiting to encounter God's love.

Remember ... in the Five Thousand, we find God can do big things even with our smallest gifts.

10

Something in the Way

They ... recognized Jesus when he broke the bread.

—LUKE 24:35 GW

Few things are more enjoyable than smelling and eating a fresh loaf of bread. One of my favorite Italian restaurants is Roncone's in Rochester, New York. This great little eatery has been open since 1937, and when I lived in upstate New York, my favorite item was the incredible Italian bread they served. I have never had any better before or since.

When my wife, Pamela, and I asked about where the bread was made, they told us, "Well, we don't bake the bread here. We buy it from a little place down the street." Since I wanted to take some home with me, I sought out the source.

We finally found the bread baker in a home with the baking ovens set up in his garage. This baker discovered what he did best and made a business out of baking incomparable breads. Roncone's managers knew they couldn't beat it, so they wisely chose this bread as a staple for their restaurant. There was just something in the way this bread was baked that made it truly special.

THE MOST UNCOMMON PROCESS

This miracle of the feeding of the Five Thousand was apparently often told and pondered by the earliest Christ followers. In fact, "this is the only miracle that all four Gospel writers saw important enough to include in their narratives."[1]

But note this: when Jesus handled bread, he always did so in one particular way and according to one method. He took four steps so methodical and predictable that at one point after his resurrection, they helped some of his followers recognize him in an otherwise unrecognizable form.

Here are the four things Jesus did with bread:

1. He *took* it.
2. He *blessed* it.
3. He *broke* it.
4. He *gave* it.

You can see the pattern unfolding in this passage:

He said to his disciples, "Have them sit down in groups of about fifty each." The disciples did so, and everyone sat down. *Taking* the five loaves and the two fish and looking up to heaven, he *gave thanks* and *broke* them. Then he *gave* them to the disciples to distribute to the people. They all ate and were satisfied, and the disciples picked up twelve basketfuls of broken pieces that were left over. (Luke 9:14–17, emphasis mine)

Did you catch it? Did you notice the take-bless-break-give order? Jesus repeated this pattern again and again in his earthly ministry and in the handling of bread. Here it is again, in Matthew's gospel: "*Taking* the five loaves and the two fish and looking up to heaven, he *gave thanks* and *broke* the loaves. Then he *gave* them to the disciples" (14:19, emphasis mine).

Church history tells us that many expositors and students of Scripture have viewed this process of how Jesus handled bread as rife with meaning. Not only did it mark a moment and create an ordinance of the church, it also revealed something of how God works in our lives as disciples.

For whatever reason, my logical assessment of how God works in our lives to shape us and grow us was always more along this order:

He *takes* us.
He *breaks* us.
He *blesses* us.
He *uses* (or *gives*) us.

I always assumed that once Jesus enters our lives in the process of redemption, salvation, and conversion, he first *takes us* or brings us to some point of humble acknowledgment of him. Also, wrapped up in that process in my mind was a *breaking* or a coming to the end of our rope or of ourselves. This glorious undoing would then lead to him laying his hand upon our lives and *blessing* us before he starts to *use* or *give* us to other people's needs. But Jesus followed a notably different pattern.

THE OTHER BREAKING

Sometimes Jesus will bless you and then tear you apart, or should I say, he will allow you to be torn apart. What we see as *tearing*, however, he sees as *breaking*. What we often view as God's taking something or some things away from us, he views as a time of giving us to others for his sake.

It has been said there is a *making* in the *breaking*. I agree, but the reverse is also true: there is a *breaking* in the *making* of God's will in our lives.

While we often want our lives to be presented to a world in need as a fully put-together, glowing example of healing and wholeness, God often wants to serve us in pieces, in broken and digestible parts of a life deeply dependent on God and his strength. Although God makes us whole in salvation, he often serves our lives as broken pieces to others.

The way God works in my life is so often counter to the way I think he is going to work. Perhaps he does it that way not just to keep me guessing but to keep me relying on his ability to lead and direct my steps instead of my ability to figure him out. Often the broken experiences we face have "happened that we might not rely on ourselves but on God, who raises the dead" (2 Cor. 1:9).

Dietrich Bonhoeffer, the brave German pastor, theologian, and anti-Nazi dissident, caught this principle and expressed it unflinchingly: "The cross is not the terrible end to an otherwise godfearing and happy life, but it meets us at the beginning of our communion with Christ. When Christ calls a man, he bids him come and die."[2]

When God breaks us, he doesn't do so to break us or our lives *apart*; rather, he wants to break us *open* to him and to the needs of others. The brokenness in our lives opens up places of humanness, connection, and community in and around us where God's presence can flow.

UNDERCOVER SAVIOR

After Jesus' resurrection, Luke records his mysterious appearance among some of his followers on the Emmaus road. In this encounter, as Christ appears in his postresurrection body, the disciples don't have a clue about who he is. After inviting him to share a meal with them, however, he does something that breaks his cover. See if you can tell what it is:

> They tried hard to keep him from leaving. They said, "Stay with us. It is nearly evening. The day is almost over." So he went in to stay with them. He joined them at the table. Then he *took* bread and *gave thanks*. He *broke it* and began to *give it* to them. Their eyes were opened, and they recognized him. But then he disappeared from their sight. . . . Then the two of them told what had happened to them on the way. They told how they had recognized Jesus when he broke the bread. (Luke 24:29–31, 35 NIRV, emphasis mine)

Their eyes were "opened." But they didn't recognize him until "he broke the bread."

The freshly baked Italian bread at Roncone's is a beautiful piece of culinary creation. It is great to look at, but only for about five seconds. I can't enjoy it until it is broken, until pieces are torn away from it, and I taste each one.

Even though our Communion plates are often filled with little pieces of broken bread, we have no record in Scripture of Jesus' blessing broken bread. We have several, however, of his blessing bread and then breaking it. Jesus *took* the bread, *blessed* it, *broke* it, and *gave* it. Our lives are bread in his hands. Once there, we, too, are blessed, broken, and given.

Remember ... in the Five Thousand, *we* are the bread that Jesus takes, blesses, breaks, and gives.

11

My Kind of King

I'm not that kind of king.

—JESUS' WORDS TO PONTIUS PILATE, JOHN 18:36 MSG

Imagine a place where all your physical needs were met 24/7, sort of an around-the-clock Super Walmart, only in this case super as in *supernatural*. This must feel better than any Medicare or HMO program ever known to man. No cards, referrals, or co-pays required. No questions asked.

But the superstore they found that day included not just a pharmacy department; it had a grocery store to beat all others. Talk about one-stop shopping! If anyone got hungry, whatever you had on hand no matter how meager a supply could be instantly multiplied into more than you could possibly need. The Five Thousand found themselves in a miraculous place. Who would ever want to leave? Can you imagine the conversations that must have taken place?

"Whoa, did you see that? That was amazing."

"He is healing everyone of everything—blind eyes, painful teeth, bad backs, vertigo, common colds, migraines, acid reflux, and who knows what else."

"Have we discovered the fountain of youth or what?"

"Talk about a social security program. I'm in!"

"Do you realize how many hours I had to work last week just to buy my family groceries? Jesus just made enough miracle food to feed an army."

"I am never going to leave this place, and if I have anything to do with it, neither is Jesus."

The biblical text, the context, and the tone of this narrative lend themselves to such a scenario as these imagined statements convey. Granted, at this stage these earliest Christ seekers discovered powerful news. They were finding how capable Christ was to provide for their needs. When you and I come into this stage of our journey toward Jesus, the motivation driving us is our need.

There was a problem, though. This gang really did not recognize Jesus as who he was; they viewed him as what they wanted him to be. How often do we do exactly the same? The Five Thousand considered Jesus not as a Savior but more as a genie in a bottle that they were determined to keep as long as possible. Read this:

After this Jesus went away to the other side of the Sea of Galilee, which is the Sea of Tiberias. And a large crowd was following him, because they saw the signs that he was doing on the sick.... When the people saw the sign that he had done, they said, "This is indeed the Prophet who is to come into the world!" *Perceiving then that they were about to come and take him by force to make him king,* Jesus withdrew again to the mountain by himself. (John 6:1–2, 14–15 ESV, emphasis mine)

While Jesus had compassionately and faithfully taught the Five Thousand about his plan and heaven itself, they had more of a mind to set up a kind of heaven on earth. They wanted their best life, and they wanted it *now*. They were preparing to seize the moment and take Jesus' future into their hands. Chaos was about to break loose. You could feel it: "They were about to come and take him by force to make him king" (v. 15 ESV).

SEIZING JESUS

What about us today? Don't we try to force our will on God instead of surrendering ourselves to his? Don't we try our best all too often to seize Jesus in a variety of ways?

Taking Jesus

Some of the vocabulary of evangelicalism could stand to be revisited. Among the phrases that need rethinking is the idea of "*taking* Jesus as our Lord and Savior." The fact is, none of us take Jesus anywhere, do we? After all, Jesus is the initiator; we are the responders in this faith relationship.

Forcing Jesus

The idea of forcing Jesus to be something we want and perhaps something other than what he intends to be is preposterous, is it not? Yet isn't it true that once we get a glimpse of what Jesus can do, our minds tend to jump ahead to what we want him to do? As a result, our prayer lists sometimes become our agendas, not his. The fascination of true followers of Jesus is not what he can do for them but what he desires to do in and through them. Jesus modeled it this way: "My food . . . is to do the will of him who sent me and to finish his work" (John 4:34).

The Russian author Leo Tolstoy stated, "There are two Gods. . . . There is the God that people generally believe in—a

God *who has to serve them* (sometimes in very refined ways, say by merely giving them peace of mind). This God does not exist. But the God whom people forget—*the God whom we all have to serve*—exists, and is the prime cause of our existence and of all that we perceive."[1]

Making Jesus

One popular phrase in evangelical Christianity has at times been that of "making Jesus Lord of our lives." The fact is, you and I don't make Jesus into anything, nor do we have the capacity to do so. Our lives are being molded, shaped, formed, and made into the image of Christ by God himself. It is not what we can make out of ourselves or what we can turn Jesus into. Jesus is making us after the image of his likeness and his will.

Following Jesus

Sometimes our "following" Jesus is not the kind of following he desires, not at all. Simply chasing after Christ for the purpose of what he can do for us or what we can get out of him misses the point. We can all too easily turn Jesus into a product we consume or, at least, the distributor of such products. When we follow Jesus we are following not a *salesman* but the *Savior*. One main purpose of his call and our following is not what it can bring to us but what it will require of us.

Following Jesus is

- not *taking* him where you want to go but following him to places he wants to go. Following Jesus will involve *journeys you never planned.*
- not *forcing* his hand but giving him yours. Following will include *surrenders you never expected.*
- not *making* him after your image, but conforming your

life to his. Following will reveal *shortcomings and sins you never knew existed.*

ANOTHER KING, ANOTHER DAY

Many years before Jesus came, God's people wanted their own kind of king for the first time. They went to the prophet Samuel and insisted on it in fact (1 Sam. 8). The people of Israel were living under a theocracy, and God was raising up leaders to guide them. But they were not satisfied. As they looked around and saw that other nations had kings, with their accompanying glories, power, and fame, the people of Israel wanted one of their own. The nation begged and argued for a king so much that possibly the worst thing that could happen did: *God gave them what they asked for.* The results were in many ways disastrous and were followed by a murderous Saul, a compromising conspirator named David, and a too-brilliant-for-his-own-good cynic named Solomon. The great nation of Israel had three kings, and many more to follow, most of whom greatly failed God. So, be careful how much you seek the kind of king you desire. God may answer your prayer as well.

Remember... in the Five Thousand, we are tempted to see Jesus as the king we *want* instead of the one we *need*.

12

Thinking with Your Stomach

Taste and see . . .

—Psalm 34:8

Lasagna is my favorite food, hands down. What meal could be more perfect than layers of homemade pasta ribboned among succulent chunks of beef, ricotta cheese, and Italian seasonings, all smothered with spicy sauce and cascading gratings of Romano cheese?

Do I sound like someone who knows my lasagna? Well, I should. When I pastored in the Boston area, I used a story about lasagna in one of my sermons. Just a few days later on a very snowy New England day, my wife and I came home and found a pan of freshly baked lasagna sitting on our porch steps. As it turned out, a seventy-year-old lady in the church named Winnie had driven several miles in the snow and up a hill to deliver it. To this day, I have never forgotten the lengths Winnie went to with that lasagna (which, by the way, was fantastically delicious!).

Sometimes the best way to turn our spirits on is to turn our stomachs off, at least for a while. This is why prayer and fasting are such vital disciplines of the Christian faith (pretty rotten of me to mention fasting right after lasagna, eh?). Fasting gives us time to temper our physical hunger and to reawaken our spiritual hungers, to master our sometimes controlling appetites with the assertion, "Man shall not live by bread alone" (Matt. 4:4 ESV).

The Five Thousand were determined to make Christ king, at least their kind of king, so after the miraculous feeding, they followed him until they found him again. By the time they caught up with him, they had traveled all the way to Capernaum or to "the other side of the sea" (John 6:22 ESV). Once they found Jesus again they asked, "Rabbi, when did you come here?" (v. 25 ESV).

But Jesus was apparently in no mood for small talk over his recent journeys and itinerary. He knew what they were up to. He answered them, "Truly, truly, I say to you, you are seeking me, not because you saw signs, but because you ate your fill of the loaves" (v. 26 ESV).

The Message states it this way: "Jesus answered, 'You've come looking for me not because you saw God in my actions but because I fed you, filled your stomachs—and for free.'"

When you find yourself in the circle of the Five Thousand in your growth in Christ, it is a wonderful place of provision. But it is also true that our primary characteristic in this place can be as consumers of God and his gifts to us.

PARTAKERS OF GOD

In a sense, the Bible invites us to consume God. After all, we are invited to "taste and see that the LORD is good" (Ps. 34:8). We are told we are "partakers of the divine nature" (2 Peter 1:4 ESV). Jesus said to his disciples, "Take, eat: this is my body, which is broken for you" (1 Cor. 11:24 KJV).

We are partakers of God, the consumers of his presence, yes. However, there is a temptation at this stage to see God as a cosmic vending machine. We can get so focused in our prayers on the gifts in the hand of God that we fail to look into his face; we can become so riveted on the gifts that we miss the Giver. But if we're not careful, though our stomachs may be full, our souls may be empty.

While Jesus affirmed that they "filled [their] stomachs," he lamented over their not seeing "God in [his] actions." Consider his words to them:

> "Do not work for the food that perishes, but for the food that endures to eternal life, which the Son of Man will give to you. For on him God the Father has set his seal." . . . So they said to him, "Then what sign do you do, that we may see and believe you? What work do you perform? Our fathers ate the manna in the wilderness; as it is written, 'He gave them bread from heaven to eat.'" Jesus then said to them, "Truly, truly, I say to you, it was not Moses who gave you the bread from heaven, but *my Father gives you the true bread from heaven.* For the bread of God is he who comes down from heaven and gives life to the world." They said to him, "Sir, give us this bread always." Jesus said to them, "I am the bread of life; whoever comes to me shall not hunger, and whoever believes in me shall never thirst." (John 6:27–35 ESV, emphasis mine)

OTHER HUNGERS

Jesus gives us a few not-to-be-missed insights in this passage:

The Five Thousand were driven by their hunger all the way to "the other side of the sea." We, too, are driven by our hungers. Consider for a moment how often you think about the next meal. If we are not thinking about our next meal, we are talking about how much we enjoyed the last one. Our culture and conversations often center on food, foodies, food trucks, food favorites, food fetishes, food shops, food flavors, food creations, health foods, Whole Foods, food restaurants, food recipes, food snacks, and even the 24/7 Food Network. Let's face it: food is often the main motivation in our lives.

There are two kinds of food, perishable and imperishable, temporal and eternal. Jesus fed the Five Thousand not simply to relieve their hunger pains and quiet their growling stomachs but also to point them to bread of another kind. He had something in mind right after his conversation with the woman at the well that he described to his disciples this way: "I have food to eat that you do not know about" (John 4:32 ESV).

Bread that comes from God "gives life to the world." It is interesting Jesus fed them and then he let them get hungry again, really hungry. When they finally found him, however, he told them what they really needed was the bread "from heaven" that "gives life to the world."

Jesus is the bread and drink you need the most. The Glorious Consumption that God wants to get us addicted to is not pizza, pasta, loaded nachos, fish tacos, lasagna, or Black Angus rib eye steaks (my personal weakness). No, he wants to tap a deeper hunger, the hunger in our hearts. This requires two things from us: open eyes and open souls; open to seeing and sensing God and the gifts of God at a deeper level. In a sense, when we walk among the Five Thousand our faith experience is a tasting faith—"taste and see that the LORD is good."

Christ followers have open eyes. Consumers merely taste the bread or food, but Christ followers taste the bread *and* see the signs. They understand a gift doesn't just fill a stomach; it reveals the Giver.

Christ followers have open souls. They recognize the importance of compassion and of offering help to those in need. However, they acknowledge that help alone is not enough. It is also important to extend the hope that is found in knowing Christ. People need help *and* hope. In fact, with hope they will often find themselves empowered to find their own help.

Christ followers don't just think with their stomachs. They think with the "mind of Christ" (1 Cor. 2:16) and find ways to give people both temporal and eternal food.

I still think of how determined Winnie was to bring us that lasagna, through the cold, the snow, the hills, and all the way up our stairs. I wonder whether I am showing the same determination in seeking out the soul food of knowing Christ and making sure others "taste and see" (Ps. 34:8).

Remember . . . in the Five Thousand, we find that Jesus is the bread and drink we most need.

13

Crazy Talk?

Does this cause you to stumble?

—Jesus, John 6:61 nasb

Jesus said some shocking things. To better understand just how shocking one of his statements was, imagine this scenario: What if your middle-school-age daughter had been attending a new club on campus for the last few months? Up to this point, you had seen and heard nothing but good about this group, about the adult leader who oversees it, and the impact it was having on your child. Then one day your child comes home and you have this conversation:

"Hey, Mom (or Dad), guess what happened at our group meeting today?" your child says.

"Not sure. What's up?" you respond.

"Well, the leader told us there is something we need to do if we want to really be connected to the group."

"Oh, yeah? What's that, volunteer at the local homeless shelter?"

"No, not exactly. Actually the leader said we had to eat his flesh and drink his blood."

"Whoa! Whaaattt!" you say. "Hold it just a minute! What in the world are you talking about?"

What would you say to your child at that point? "You are never going back to that group again!" or "Give me the name of the leader who said that!" or "I'm calling the police!"

The teaching Jesus used following the feeding of the Five Thousand must have been alarming to them. While looking at the hungry crowds of Five Thousand who had followed him all the way to Capernaum in hopes of a second miracle meal and many others, Jesus said, "I am the bread of life. Your fathers ate the manna in the wilderness, and they died. This is the bread that comes down from heaven, so that one may eat of it and not die. I am the living bread that came down from heaven. If anyone eats of this bread, he will live forever. And the bread that I will give for the life of the world is my flesh" (John 6:48–51 ESV).

By this time, you might expect Jesus would have clarified the imagery or the metaphorical significance of his words. Michael Card described it this way:

> If ever an explanation was called for from Jesus it is now. A few words might have calmed them down and helped them understand His horrific statement: "My flesh is true food, and My blood is true drink."
>
> John does not record the response of the mob for us. Perhaps it was best left unsaid. . . .
>
> "Does this cause you to stumble?" Jesus asked. . . . When Jesus speaks of stumbling . . . the word in Greek is scandalize; it comes from the noun *scandalon* [i.e., the word from which we derive the English word *scandal*].[1]

SHOCKING WORDS

No subtle imagery here. Jesus' words were shocking to them and even scandalous. He became even more vivid and graphic in his statements:

> Truly, truly, I say to you, unless you eat the flesh of the Son of Man and drink his blood, you have no life in you. Whoever feeds on my flesh and drinks my blood has eternal life, and I will raise him up on the last day. For my flesh is true food, and my blood is true drink. Whoever feeds on my flesh and drinks my blood abides in me, and I in him. As the living Father sent me, and I live because of the Father, so whoever feeds on me, he also will live because of me. This is the bread that came down from heaven, not like the bread the fathers ate, and died. Whoever feeds on this bread will live forever. (John 6:53–58 ESV)

We can only imagine the responses from the Five Thousand who had so recently tasted of Jesus' miracle food and healings:

> "Jesus, you're not making it any easier to keep following you."
> "This is getting really weird."
> "You don't really mean that, do you?"
> "Jesus, maybe you're the one who needs something to eat."
> "That's just crazy talk."

Jesus' approach seemed to be the very opposite of what we often take in our pulpits, preachings, and teachings today. Don't we often try to smooth out the path to Christ and make it simpler and easier to follow him?

THE TEST OF TRUST

The hard words of Jesus on this occasion became a dividing point among the disciples. In the earliest years of the church, many Romans had great disdain for Christians because of mistaken rumors of cannibalism. When it came to following Christ, this moment and these hard words divided the men from the boys.

There were other occasions when God and his leaders said such hard words that only one thing could have empowered the hearers to stay and to follow through: faith. Similar moments occurred in the Bible when

- God told Abraham to leave the land he knew and go to a place he did not,
- God told Moses to use his stammering lips to demand Pharaoh let his people go, and
- God told a virgin she would bear his Son.

Such moments require the greatest miracle of all—the one that takes place in our souls and in our minds, the miracle of faith.

TROUBLE SWALLOWING?

Following Jesus requires faith, and that is not a human ability we muster up. No, the Scripture clearly teaches that our faith is a "gift of God" (Eph. 2:8). It is a divine enablement. The Bible says every person has been given "the measure of faith" (Rom. 12:3 KJV). So, in this moment when some allowed faith to flow, others did not or would not. Instead, they found this bread hard to swallow:

Many among his disciples heard this and said, "This is tough teaching, too tough to swallow." Jesus sensed his disciples were having a hard time with this and said, "Does this throw you completely? What would happen if you saw the Son of Man ascending to where he came from? The Spirit can make life. Sheer muscle and willpower don't make anything happen. Every word I've spoken to you is a Spirit-word, and so it is life-making. But some of you are resisting, refusing to have any part in this." (Jesus knew from the start that some weren't going to risk themselves with him. He knew also who would betray him.) He went on to say, "This is why I told you earlier that no one is capable of coming to me on his own. You get to me only as a gift from the Father." After this a lot of his disciples left. They no longer wanted to be associated with him. (John 6:60–67 MSG)

The manna and miracles compelled people to follow Jesus, yet they led to some things people never expected. Once he offered more of what they wanted; now he told them what they truly needed. Accepting his words required discernment and insight. He presented bread and wine as more than sustenance; they were images of a Savior who was prepared to give his body and blood for their sakes on a cross.

What about you and the hard words of Jesus? Are you resisting them, refusing them, or receiving them? Remember, his words "are full of the Spirit and life" (v. 63). Jesus' words are more than pious platitudes. They are as real as were the flesh on his bones and the blood in his veins. How real are they in your life today?

Remember . . . in the Five Thousand, Jesus' words and ways may not always make sense to us at first.

14

*Life*Words

*The words that I have spoken to
you are spirit and are life.*

—Jesus, John 6:63 nasb

God wants to breathe a word into your soul. I'm convinced of it. It happened to people in the Bible. It happened to the Five Thousand. It can also happen to you.

God has written his words in a book, the Bible, and he wants to write his words on your heart. When God highlights a passage of Scripture in someone's life, it marks a specific moment with a specific insight from his heart to theirs. Such moments are transforming and needed. Jesus said, "Man shall not live by bread alone, but by every word that proceeds from the mouth of God" (Matt. 4:4 nkjv).

There is a great difference between casually reading a Bible passage and truly sensing God speaking those words to your soul.

God wants our eyes to read the words he has left for us, and he wants to breathe one of them upon our souls. I call these *Life*Words.

BORED WITH THE BIBLE?

*Life*Word moments occur when a powerful insight is planted into your soul. You swallow a truth capsule containing time-release nutrients, each awaiting its ordained moment of effect. In those times, I believe God's Word is "sharper than any two-edged sword" (Heb. 4:12 KJV), and I can feel it at work in me. I sense the razored edges of both biblical blades severing the sins in my life, penetrating my soul, and carving out the image of Christ within me.

A. W. Tozer stretched our thinking about God's words:

> The Bible is the written word of God, and because it is written it is confined and limited by the necessities of ink and paper and leather. The Voice of God, however, is alive and free as the sovereign God is free. . . . God's word in the Bible can have power only because it corresponds to God's word in the universe. It is the present Voice which makes the written Word all-powerful. Otherwise it would lie locked in slumber within the covers of a book.[1]

THE WORD *WORD*

Two primary Greek words are used in the New Testament for *word*. One is *logos*, used most often, some seven hundred times, to refer to the word of God in its general form. The other word, used only seventy times, is *rhema*. A *rhema* is a word specifically spoken or given for a particular situation or need. While a *logos* is a word that is general in its sweep, a *rhema* is specific and pointed in its purpose.[2] Our souls and lives need both.

There are times when the written word on a page becomes the spoken word in my soul. I do more than read it; I hear it. In those moments, the Word becomes a "lamp for my feet, a light on my path" (Ps. 119:105).

Unfortunately some Bible teachers today have misinterpreted the concept of *rhema*. They have mistakenly considered person-to-person utterances, whether biblically based or not, to be the equivalent of a *rhema* or *Life*Word. Such teaching is an erroneous overstatement.

A *Life*Word (or *rhema*) is a biblical passage that takes on a strategic personal application in our lives. The apostle Paul put it this way: "All Scripture is God-breathed and is useful for teaching, rebuking, correcting and training in righteousness, so that the man of God may be thoroughly equipped for every good work" (2 Tim. 3:16–17).

Two respected biblical scholars expressed the significance of *rhema* words (for example, *Life*Words) as distinct from *logos*. W. E. Vine stated, "The significance of *rhema* (as distinct from *logos*) is exemplified in the injunction to take 'the sword of the Spirit, which is the word of God,' Eph. 6:17; here the reference is not to the whole Bible as such, but to *the individual scripture which the Spirit brings to our remembrance for use in time of need.*"[3] F. F. Bruce, in like manner, asserted, "The 'word' (*rhema*) is that utterance of God *appropriate to the occasion* which the Spirit, so to speak, puts into the believer's hand to be wielded as a sword which will put his spiritual assailants to flight."[4]

A *Life*Word for a Lost Soul

Jesus breathed *Life*Words over people's souls. When he spoke to the woman taken into adultery, for instance, think of all the negative words that surrounded her. The "religious" people in her community said things like: "This woman was taken in adultery"

(John 8:4 KJV), and "[She] should be stoned" (v. 5 KJV). I am sure she heard many more condemning words in her life.

But Jesus approached her not with condemnation but with forgiveness. And after he showed his grace and kindness, he did not call her to a public place of humiliation; instead he sent her off with a *Life*Word: "Neither do I condemn you; go, and from now on sin no more" (John 8:11 ESV).

To the ears of her accusers, these words were undeserved and inappropriate. Yet within the recesses of her soul, they must have felt like a soothing ointment. They would become the voice of God to her for the rest of her life. How many times must she have recounted them afterward? They were God's *rhema*, a *Life*Word just for her.

WONDER BREAD

In John's account of the feeding of the Five Thousand (6:1–15), the event led to something. The physical feeding of mouths pointed to a more important meal, the bread of God's Word. So many who heard Jesus speak of eating his flesh and drinking his blood took him literally and stumbled, yet Jesus described his words as "Spirit and life" (v. 63). He challenged the followers not to stumble over what he said but to hear and see the Spirit of his words, to catch the underlying message. He challenges us to do the same:

> "Every word I've spoken to you is a Spirit-word, and so it is life-making. But some of you are resisting, refusing to have any part in this." (Jesus knew from the start that some weren't going to risk themselves with him. He knew also who would betray him.) He went on to say, "This is why I told you earlier that no one is capable of coming to me on his own. You get to me only as a gift from the Father." After

this a lot of his disciples left. They no longer wanted to be associated with him. (vv. 63–67 MSG)

The words of Jesus draw us closer to him and call us to deny self, to place our will and wishes on the cross with Christ. We must be aware and be careful. While the barrier to our development beyond the Crowds is our unbelief, *a barrier to our development at this place of the Five Thousand is our selfishness.*

The surgery of spiritual transformation will not occur in our lives without the primary surgical instrument of God's word: his general words to us all and the ones he illumines to us by his Holy Spirit that become *Life*Words. The walk of faith will mean not only meditating on those words but marinating in them as well!

Remember . . . in the Five Thousand, we realize what Jesus says are more than mere words; they are Spirit and life.

PART 2

Encountering Christ, the Lord

The Seventy

Serving the Purposes of Christ

"When I heard him sending out workers to join in
his cause and to engage in serving others, I knew I
wanted to be a part. That day as he approached me
and the other sixty-nine, I knew this work could
change my life, and it may change so many others, even entire villages and towns. When he gave
us his words of commission, I could tell by his
tone just how vital the mission would be. Putting
my faith to work is something I am comfortable
doing, and if these new teachings can affect other
places as they have my hometown, it will be a
blazing fire of sweeping change. When he called,
he said it's time; get moving now and don't worry
about bags, purses, or sandals. The work is waiting; it's time to up and go!"

15

Follow, Follow, Follow

"Come, follow me," Jesus said.

—MATTHEW 4:19

Long before Twitter repopularized, and in some ways re-defined, the term *follow*, it was said and sung to rapt audiences in the Broadway production and the Hollywood film *The Wizard of Oz*. The enchanting story depicts the dream of a young girl, Dorothy, who becomes frustrated with her family and gets caught up in an adventure with three characters on a similar quest: a tin man, a scarecrow, and a cowardly lion.

The path set before the troupe of Oz travelers to reach their supposed answers is a yellow brick road. Their only directive is to "follow, follow, follow the yellow brick road."

When we follow Jesus to this place of the Seventy, *our primary motivation is purpose.* This was also the motivation of those original

Seventy. We move from *hearing* about this kingdom of God to *entering into its work*. In our growth in Christ, *the Seventy represent the place where we are drawn to Jesus' mission*. We are compelled by what he says and drawn toward what he does.

Essential to Jesus' mission is that we follow him. Jesus went to great lengths to clarify and define the word *follow*. It was one of which he wanted his disciples to be ever so clear.

The *Following* Questions

In Luke's gospel, just before Jesus sent out the Seventy[1] to do ministry and prepare people for his upcoming visits, he took time with a few of them to carefully redefine the word *follow*.

> As they were walking along the road, a man said to him, "I will follow you wherever you go." Jesus replied, "Foxes have dens and birds have nests, but the Son of Man has no place to lay his head." He said to another man, "Follow me." But he replied, "Lord, first let me go and bury my father." Jesus said to him, "Let the dead bury their own dead, but you go and proclaim the kingdom of God." Still another said, "I will follow you, Lord; but first let me go back and say goodbye to my family." Jesus replied, "No one who puts a hand to the plow and looks back is fit for service in the kingdom of God." (Luke 9:57–62)

Jesus in essence asked of three would-be followers, including (1) Where's your home? (2) Who's your Daddy? (yes, you read that right!), and (3) What's your priority?

In the first scenario, someone confidently said to Jesus, "I will follow you wherever you go" (v. 57). This would-be follower implied he was so devoted to Jesus that he was prepared to go everywhere Jesus went. Jesus responded that while "foxes have dens and birds have nests" to call home, "the Son of Man has no place to lay his head" (v. 58).

The second would-be follower seemed a bit more hesitant than the first. This individual did not volunteer as did the first person; Jesus issued an invitation to him to "follow me." His response came with a qualification: "Lord, first let me go and bury my father" (v. 59). Jesus' answer seemed as abrupt as the first person's boast: "Let the dead bury their own dead" (v. 60). Wow! That was a bit strong, wasn't it?

The fact is, the Seventy would be given the high privilege of soon proclaiming "the kingdom of God has come near to you" (Luke 10:9). In light of the moment and all it meant, while the would-be follower's earthly father was fading from the scene, Christ wanted to move his focus and loyalties to the eternal Father.

The final *following* lesson came from one who in essence said, "I'll follow you, Lord, but first I need to say a few good-byes back home." Consider Jesus' response: "No one, after putting his hand to the plow and looking back, is fit for the kingdom of God" (Luke 9:62 NASB).

Jesus sounded more like a drill sergeant than a devoted pastor, didn't he? His purpose was not to comfort his disciples but to challenge them to the depths.[2]

On this journey of growing as followers and disciples of Christ, we must realize God has an intended goal in this process. We work for him, but mostly he is working in us. We are being transformed. As God works to change the world, he starts by changing our world. Dallas Willard wrote, "His objective is eventually to bring all of human life on earth under the direction of his wisdom, goodness, and power, as part of God's eternal plan for the universe. . . . We must make no mistake about it. In thus sending out his trainees, he set afoot a *perpetual world revolution*: one that is still in process and will continue until God's will is done on earth as it is in heaven."[3]

DIMINISHING JESUS?

Too often we live with a kind of Jesus in mind who is nothing like the one revealed in Scripture. We soften him and make him after our own image, wants, or biases. Another Dorothy, the late renowned Christian writer Dorothy Sayers, said it well:

> The people who hanged Christ never, to do them justice, accused Him of being a bore—on the contrary, they thought Him too dynamic to be safe. It has been left for later generations to muffle up that shattering personality and surround Him with an atmosphere of tedium. We have very efficiently pared the claws of the Lion of Judah, certified Him 'meek and mild,' and recommended Him as a fitting household pet for pale curates and pious old ladies.[4]

When Jesus sent out the Seventy, he showed us he wanted (and wants) much more than constituents, consumers, or club members; he called colaborers to join in his kingdom work. The promises of Christ's call are astounding; the demands at times are shocking. When he said, "Follow me," Jesus was looking hard into the eyes of three would-be followers and asking them:

"Where's your home?"
"Who's your Daddy?"
"What's your priority?"

He asks us the same things today. The answers he sought from the three would-be followers, though never stated by any of them, were clearly implied:

"Yes, Jesus, you are my true home. The center of operations for my life and ministry is now you."

"Jesus, you are the everlasting Father. My loyalties have now changed, and you are first and foremost."

"Jesus, your kingdom is my priority one. I will no longer assume what I need to do next; instead I will humbly ask and faithfully obey."

- As it turns out in Oz, *following* meant skipping down a shiny sidewalk;
- on Twitter, *following* means clicking a key on your computer; and
- for Christ, *following* means moving at the impulse of his call, at his word, in his direction, and nowhere else.

Remember . . . in the Seventy, we follow Christ
to the places of working and serving.

16

Do, for You

*Work willingly at whatever you do, as
though you were working for the Lord.*

—Colossians 3:23 nlt

Jesus' ministry was catching fire in the culture by the time he
sent out the Seventy. Things were really coming together. A team
had been trained and was being commissioned. Jesus "sent [the
Seventy out] two by two ahead of him to every town and place
where he was about to go" (Luke 10:1). They were the front men
for Jesus' ministry.

As we are learning, the Seventy were those who followed
Jesus to *the place of working and serving* (Luke 10:1–24). At that
point, the stakes were high; the promises grand; and the results
astounding. Just read some of the headlines:

The harvest is plentiful. (v. 2)

Go! I am sending you out like lambs among wolves. (v. 3)

Heal the sick. (v. 9)

Tell them, "The kingdom of God has come near to you."
(v. 9)

I have given you authority . . . to overcome all the power of
the enemy. (v. 19)

Essentially Jesus was saying, nothing will harm you (vv.
3–18).

My Journey into the Seventy

After walking in a relationship with Christ for about a year, I
was suddenly somewhat thrust into the Seventy. My family and
I were attending a new church we were excited about. The worship was joyous, the sermons convicting and full of passion, and
so many of the people so welcoming and passionate about Jesus.
We were soaking it all up.

The youth service was always on Sunday nights, and I rarely
missed. The one night I chose not to attend because of excessive
homework at my high school, something unexpected happened.
I was voted in as president of the youth group.

The next morning the assistant pastor of the church called
me and said, "Guess what? You're the new youth group president."

I asked, "What does that mean?"

He said, "Well, that means you are in charge of everything
in the youth group. You will plan *all* the youth services, lead worship in them, and plan and lead *all* the various youth events and
activities."

I said something like, "Really? Are you sure I can do all that?
I'm a pretty new believer."

Whether or not I was prepared, I suddenly was thrust into

the work of the Lord at my home church. Even though I was arguably in way over my head, the encouragement and support I received from the church staff and parents over that next year were incredible. It was sort of a baptism of fire into ministry, but honestly few things have ever fired me up personally as did that open door.

THE SEVENTY

The Seventy represent a major step in a follower's journey with Jesus. Consider this: the Lord brings us through *the place of watching and listening*, from within the Crowds, where we get our first glimpses of Jesus, his words, and his works. Next, he leads us to *the places of receiving from God*, where we are fed, even healed and nourished by his Spirit, among the Five Thousand. Then, he calls us into *the places of service*, among the Seventy, into the privilege of investing our gifts and energy in the works that matter most to him.

When you come to this place in your journey with Jesus, as did the Seventy, you have learned that *his works* are worth watching and considering, *his words* are worth hearing and heeding, *his gifts* are worth asking for and enjoying, and you start to realize something else. You recognize that thus far in your journey you have been much more on the *receiving end* of this arrangement. Suddenly, you begin to wonder about something else.

You begin to ask yourself questions:

What gifts do I have to offer the Lord?
How can I serve others the way others have served me?
What ministry can I contribute to in my local church and
*   community?*
What missionary or missions agency can I invest my life in?
What portion of my income should I invest in God's work?

*How can I help my pastor and church leaders build and grow
the church?*
How can I become a more effective witness for Jesus?

John Calvin recognized the importance of following Christ
to places of service: "For as the surest source of destruction to
men is to obey themselves, so the only haven of safety is to have
no other will, no other wisdom, than to follow the Lord wherever
he leads. Let this, then, be the first step, to abandon ourselves,
and devote the whole energy of our minds to the service of God."[1]

There is a danger, however, of staying solely in this ring of relationship to the Lord too long, in the place of the Seventy. While
we can grow closer to Christ by serving him and working for him,
we must add more to this experience. We must avoid the temptation to work as if we are earning God's grace. No, his grace to
us, his love and forgiveness, is an entirely free gift. He gives grace
unconditionally. But he calls us to invest our lives and abilities in
service to him and to relentlessly pursue intimacy with him.

Ultimately we serve God not because we want to be forgiven but because we are forgiven. Accordingly, we are not saved
because we teach a Sunday school class. On the contrary, we
teach that class or serve cups of refreshing water to the thirsty
because we are saved. There is a vast difference between *working
for* Jesus Christ and *knowing him*.

Dallas Willard wrote, "The way of Jesus Christ is a way
of *firsthand interaction*—knowing by acquaintance—direct
awareness of him and his kingdom. . . . you can't really sustain
a kingdom life . . . without such interaction with the King. And
such an interaction with God is the most precious thing available
to any human being."[2]

The works of service that truly please God are the ones that
flow out of our love relationship with him. Oswald Chambers
said, "The lasting value of our public service for God is

measured by the depth of the intimacy of our private times of fellowship and oneness with Him."[3]

How far are you willing to follow Jesus Christ? To the places of *watching* and *listening*? To the places of *feeding* and *receiving*? Or to the places of *working* and *serving*? In a sense, as we move from one of these experiences of growth to another, we don't leave those earlier experiences; we add to what we have learned and become more "complete" in Christ. As Paul wrote, "We proclaim Him, admonishing every man and teaching every man with all wisdom, so that we may present every man *complete* in Christ" (Col. 1:28 NASB, emphasis mine).

God is looking for more than mere workers. If workers fully fit the bill, he could have created another host of angels. No, when God made human beings and walked among them, he was looking for *lovers.*

When a man asked Jesus to name the "greatest commandment," he pulled no punches in conveying his passion: "'Love the Lord your God with all your heart and with all your soul and with all your mind.' This is the first and greatest commandment. And the second is like it: 'Love your neighbor as yourself'" (Matt. 22:36–39). Tragically, too many people serve aspects of God's agenda but have not learned to embrace his loving heart and nature in their lives. In God's kingdom, we serve as a way to show our love for God and toward humanity for Jesus' sake.

Loving is the goal; serving is a means of fulfilling the goal.

Remember... in the Seventy, we discover we are not just called to do *something* but to do it for *Someone.*

17

Don't Miss the Wow!

Joy is the serious business of Heaven.[1]

—C. S. LEWIS

"Look up and say, 'Wow!'" I encouraged my three-year-old daughter, Kandace, to lift her head and enjoy the view everyone else around us seemed to be missing. While my wife and our other three children were busy Christmas shopping, Kandace and I were in the middle of the panoramic atrium of the CambridgeSide Galleria mall in Boston, Massachusetts. My job for the afternoon was to take care of my daughter and free up the rest of my family to shop.

It wasn't too long before my eyes moved from the frantic crowds around me to the decorations above me. After scanning the gorgeous garlands, ribbons, and lights strung along the frames of the windowed skylights high above our heads, I thought I would invite my daughter to join in my diversion.

"Hey, Kandace!"

"Huh," she said, looking at me.

"Look up and say, 'Wow!'" I told her.

Kandace moved her head and turned her eyes away from the bustling crowds of shoppers and upward to the colorful sights.

"Wow!" she said as she surveyed the array of reds, whites, and greens.

I smiled at my daughter's simple enthusiasm and started to ask her a few questions as we admired the decorations:

"How high do you think those lights and windows are, Kandace?"

"Who put all those way up there?"

"Who cleans all those windows?"

"How do they get up there to do it?"

"Would you go up there and do that?"

"Would you do it for a dollar? A hundred dollars?"

Her jaw dropped as she kept looking up and as she pondered my barrage of questions. She had two answers for me: "I don't know!" was one. Then to my inquiry about her doing the windows, "Noooooooo! Uh-uh!" She shook her head vigorously and took another drink from her sippy cup.

Within a few short minutes our minds had moved from watching the multitudes of stressed and scurrying shoppers to beholding the wonders of the creativity and colors displayed above. The exercise lightened the moments, brought smiles to our faces, kept us talking, and made the waiting time pass a bit faster.

WORTH THE WOW?

Later that day when I told my wife about our Wow moment at the mall, it occurred to me that the experience was a metaphor of life. In the name of Christmas, a season set aside to remember the wonder of the incarnation, the masses were instead engaging the holiday by stressing over the right gift, the right size, the right color, and the right price. Most of us have done the same.

Worship itself is all about looking up and saying, "Wow!" and honoring God amid the busy buzz of life. When we enter the experience of the Seventy, *the focal point becomes our role in God's work.* This is an exciting place and experience. There are few things as exhilarating as being used by God to serve and bless others. Honestly, I believe it is far more impacting than being blessed by God.

Sometimes as Christians, however, we can get so focused on the work of the Lord that we overlook the Lord of the work. No, I didn't coin the phrase nor can I find who did, but it sure strikes an all-too-familiar chord, doesn't it? This is the mistake seemingly made by the Seventy whom Jesus sent out as a front team of ministers for him.

When the Seventy returned they brought an enthusiastic report to Jesus: "The seventy returned with joy, saying, 'Lord, even the demons are subject to us in Your name'" (Luke 10:17 NASB). The Seventy "returned with joy." But what were they so joyful about? They made that quite clear: "Even the demons are subject to us in Your name." Somehow the experience of evil forces bowing to their entrance on the various scenes "in [Jesus'] name" was astounding, even exhilarating.

But from Jesus' perspective they were missing the most important part. He said to them, "I saw Satan fall like lightning from heaven. Behold, I have given you authority to tread on serpents and scorpions, and over all the power of the enemy, and nothing shall hurt you. Nevertheless, do not rejoice in this, that the spirits are subject to you, but rejoice that your names are written in heaven" (vv. 18–20 ESV).

Jesus affirmed the powerful ministry of the Seventy. He affirmed that their work was supercharged with God's "lightning" power and protection. To Jesus, however, the power was a by-product. What matters much more is the Person who fills us with that power. The lesson here of prioritizing the Person over the power is reminiscent of a similar admonition to the Five Thousand of seeing beyond the gifts to the Giver. His invitation here was an important reminder to us, even a command: "Do not rejoice in this, that the spirits are subject to you, but rejoice that your names are written in heaven" (v. 20 ESV).

If Jesus' invitation to the Crowds was, "Come to me, all you who are weary and burdened, and I will give you rest" (Matt. 11:28), then *his invitation to the Five Thousand* could have been, "What do you want me to do for you?" (Mark 10:51), and *his invitation to the Seventy* was most certainly, "Rejoice that your names are written in heaven" (Luke 10:20 ESV).

WORK AND WORSHIP

The rest of Luke 10 reaffirms what matters most, and two stories make it clear. First of all, right after Jesus affirmed that the top two commandments are loving God and loving your neighbor as yourself, he defined who our neighbor is by telling the parable of the good Samaritan (vv. 25–37). This story asserts the importance of reaching beyond selfish concerns and social stigmas to help someone struggling or in need.

Then, just about the time we may start to think Jesus was making social concern or social justice the preeminent part of our faith, he led us and the disciples to the home of Mary and Martha and reaffirmed what is most important: loving God. He taught it in principle and then showed it applied in life through the contrast of Martha and Mary:

Now as they went on their way, Jesus entered a village. And a woman named Martha welcomed him into her house. And she had a sister called Mary, who sat at the Lord's feet and listened to his teaching. But Martha was distracted with much serving. And she went up to him and said, "Lord, do you not care that my sister has left me to serve alone? Tell her then to help me." But the Lord answered her, "Martha, Martha, you are anxious and troubled about many things, but one thing is necessary. *Mary has chosen the good portion, which will not be taken away from her.*" (vv. 38–42 ESV, emphasis mine)

Martha worked to serve Christ, but she certainly missed the Wow; she missed the importance of connecting with Christ, of relationship and worship. Instead she complained to Jesus: "Lord, do you not care . . ."

Ever done the same thing?

Although work is vital, the overflow of a life lived in a love relationship with Jesus is "the good portion." Don't just "whistle while you work"; worship while you work. That's what Jesus was telling the disciples.

At the mall in Boston, I completed the job of watching Kandace and the shopping bags that day, but I am so glad we took a little time to look up above the busy crowds. So many were in too much of a hurry to see the beautiful decorations above.

By all means engage the work and service of God, as did the Seventy, but make sure in the midst of it that you don't miss the Wow!

Remember . . . in the Seventy, while we do the work, it is essential for us not to miss the Wow!

18

The Locker Room Speech

The kingdom of God has come near.

—LUKE 10:9

Locker room speeches are a coach's last chance to fire up the team just before a game. Few events in sports history have been more climactic and inspiring than the 1980 U.S. hockey team's win over the perennially winning Russian team in Lake Placid, New York. People who understood the sport thought it impossible for any team other than the Russians to win the gold in those Olympics. The film *Miracle* recounts the locker room speech given to the underdogs by Coach Herb Brooks just before they took to the ice. The lines were short, determined, and stirring. Here are just a few:

> Great moments . . . are born from great opportunity. And that's what you have here. . . . You were born to be hockey

players. Every one of you. And you were meant to be here tonight. . . .

This is your time. Now go out there and take it. . . .

When you pull on that jersey, you represent yourself and your teammates. And the name on the front is . . . a lot more important than the one on the back![1]

The plan of God for reaching a world desperately in need of his love included the Crowds, the Five Thousand, and ultimately Jesus' selection of the Twelve; it also involved a front team of the Seventy. And in the Seventy *our primary characteristic is that of colaborers.* We are called and empowered to serve God and his mission *together.*

The Seventy were sent out as the front men to help prep the communities that Christ was soon to visit, yet we cannot assume they were well-developed disciples of Jesus. As we read in the last chapter, their final report to Jesus drew more of a rebuke from him than an affirmation because of their faulty view. Nevertheless Jesus turned those novices loose to help spread the word.

Sometimes as church leaders, we put too many controls on the Christian growth process and the nurturing of witnesses in our communities. With all the compromises and indiscretions of the woman at the well, Jesus did not assign her to a twelve-week training course before turning her loose to share her faith. No, this woman went immediately to Jericho and told people what Jesus had done for her. Because of her boldness—and perhaps because of her previous scandalous notoriety—"many of the Samaritans from that town believed in [Jesus] because of the woman's testimony" (John 4:39). I wonder whether any of us would have given someone so new to Christ and of such ill repute the same freedom to speak for Christ.

Perhaps more of our sermons, small-group Bible studies,

and mentoring sessions need to adopt the tone and dynamics of the locker room. While we all could stand to be drawn deeper into the wonderful truths and freeing insights of Scripture, we also desperately need to be called into the work and mission of God. Yes, we need to read the text, but we also need to be rallied to the cause of Christ. The biblical narrative is chock-full of dynamic coaching sessions:

> God told Joshua, "Be strong and of good courage . . . for the LORD your God is with you" (Josh. 1:9 NKJV).
> Paul told Timothy, "God has not given us a spirit of fear, but of power and of love and of a sound mind" (2 Tim. 1:7 NKJV).
> The angel told Gideon, "The LORD is with you, mighty warrior" (Judg. 6:12).
> The armor bearer told Jonathan, "Do all that you have in mind. . . . I am with you heart and soul" (1 Sam. 14:7).

COACH JESUS

Just before sending his NFL (Newbie Faithworker League) team onto the field, Jesus gave them a locker room talk of his own. Can't you just see them huddled around him and hanging on his every word? Standing strong and determined, Jesus looked them straight in the eye. He poured his passion into them. He fired them up for the big game and all it would require. He had vital themes to convey:

There Is a Massive Need Around You

"The harvest truly is great" (Luke 10:2 NKJV). The Seventy faced a world in such great need; so do we today. You don't have to look far to recognize that people all around us need Jesus.

There Is a Meager Workforce with You

"The laborers are few" (v. 2 NKJV). It seems the Pareto Principle of 20 percent of the people doing 80 percent of the work still holds true often today, doesn't it?[2] The question is: Are you in that vital minority?

There Is a Dangerous Calling Before You

"I am sending you out like lambs among wolves" (v. 3). Jesus arguably lived a dangerous life and engaged a dangerous mission, rescuing a world in rebellion against God. As John Piper said, in the walk of faith, "risk is right."[3]

So here's the plan from Jesus:

TRAVEL LIGHT. "Carry neither money bag, knapsack, nor sandals" (v. 4 NKJV). To follow Jesus farther we have to lay aside the things that will weigh us down and hold us back in our pursuit of him and his work. What's holding you back in your passionate pursuit of Jesus?

STAY FOCUSED. "Greet no one along the road" (v. 4 NKJV). Life is full of so many opportunities—some that can help us on our journey of faith and many others that can slow us down. We must determine with every opportunity, is it a divine appointment or a diversion?

CULTIVATE THE FAITHFUL ONES. "Remain in the same house" (v. 7 NKJV). Carl Lentz, pastor of Hillsong Church in New York City, said, "Show me your five closest friends and I'll show you where you will be in five years."[4] While we do God's work, it is vital we do life with people determined to follow him closely.

MINISTER TO PEOPLE'S FELT NEEDS. "Heal the sick" (v. 9 NKJV). While we strive to bring people the hope that comes from knowing Christ, we are called to continually serve the real felt needs of their lives.

PROCLAIM THE GREAT DAY HAS COME. Let people know a new King is coming and that "the kingdom of God has come near" (v. 9 NKJV). With excitement, Jesus was calling the Seventy to proclaim this was a moment not to be missed.

How about you? Could you use a pep talk in your faith walk? If so, back up and reread the Coach Jesus section. This time, don't read it as what he said to the Seventy more than two thousand years ago. Read it as what the Spirit of God is saying to you this very moment. Let these words become your *Life*Words. After all, they were written then so you would read them now.

Jesus has called you into the high privilege and great responsibility of doing the work of the Lord. That's an opportunity not to be missed. Now's the time.

Today.

"The kingdom of God is near."

Remember ... in the Seventy, we find that Jesus guides us and that his words actually coach us.

19

Thank You, George

Not so with you.

—Matthew 20:26

The best gift George Washington ever gave to the country he fought to help found was not leading the Continental army or becoming the first president of the United States; it was how he handled the power once he entered office. George was reluctant to run a second term, and he refused to run for a third, against popular sentiments. His decision established limits to the powerful role of president early on.

As I mentioned, when the Seventy returned from their ministry tour of the towns and villages Jesus was about to visit, they were pumped, psyched, stirred, excited, enthused, and full of motivation: "When the seventy-two disciples returned, they joyfully reported to him, 'Lord, even the demons obey us when we use your name!'" (Luke 10:17 NLT).

Power. Our culture is obsessed with it. Our lives are affected by it. And yes, our churches are exposed to it. Just think for a moment of how much power permeates our lives. Power lunches, power ties, power drinks, power plays, power moves, power brokers, power books, power bars, power tools, power psychology, self-empowerment. Hey, even Power Rangers. (Remember them?) These themes and more fill our offices, companies, and bookshelves in America. Power is big business.

THE LOVE OF POWER

Napoleon, the emperor of France, was so obsessed with power, he wrote, "I love power . . . as a musician loves his violin, for the tones I can bring forth, for the chords and harmonies."[1] Others throughout history have been less enchanted with power, however. Lord Acton is often quoted as saying, "Power tends to corrupt, and absolute power corrupts absolutely."[2]

In Jesus' day, power was a central issue. The primary power threat to the Jewish people had become Rome. Many Jews regarded Roman culture as a power threat; the Romans, rather, preferred to view their influence as progress. The Pharisees perceived power as a chance to legislate righteousness among the populace in the form of tedious laws and traditions. The Zealots, on the contrary, were tired of talk; they were determined to fight fire with fire in the name of God, and they sought to overpower the oppressors of their day with the sword.

Jesus issued a warning to the power brokers of his day, including the religious leaders: "Woe to you Pharisees, because you love the most important seats in the synagogues and greetings in the marketplaces" (Luke 11:43). He also issued a challenge to the men who followed him: "Not so with you. Instead, whoever wants to become great among you must be your servant" (Matt. 20:26).

THE POWER OF LOVE

Christ confronted a society obsessed with power with something more powerful than power itself. *Love*. But not just love, a new kind of love (Greek, *agape*).[3] This force of love so powerfully touched and changed the heart of the apostle John, that his name changed from a son of thunder (Mark 3:17 KJV) to John the "Beloved Disciple."[4] John wrote about this power: "God is love [*agape*]. Whoever lives in love lives in God, and God in them.... There is no fear in love. But perfect love drives out fear, because fear has to do with punishment. The one who fears is not made perfect in love" (1 John 4:16–19).

"God is love." That is perhaps one of the shortest sentences in the Bible and yet so sweeping in its meaning and significance. Few words are ascribed to God in so clear-cut a fashion as this one. It is as if God and love are interchangeable and synonymous. John the Beloved invites us to get to know God by getting to know love, to get to know love by getting to know God.

Power was arguably an essential part of Jesus' earthly ministry. Jesus displayed his power, however, only when it had a love purpose connected to it. Think about it! His healings were his demonstrations of love. He did not administer them en masse; he approached those in need one-on-one. When he multiplied the fish and loaves of bread, his love saw five thousand hungry stomachs and was determined to fill them.

SHOW ME THE POWER!

The Pharisees repeatedly asked Jesus to "show them a sign" of his power, and Jesus' response was emphatic: "A wicked and adulterous generation looks for a miraculous sign [of power]" (Matt. 16:1–4).

Our lives are constantly filled with opportunities and

challenges that call upon us to act with power or love. Power seeks to control; love seeks to serve. Moment by moment, every one of us must decide what will motivate our actions, reactions, and responses. Those moments occur when your spouse reminds you that it's your turn to change the diapers, when the kids spill their milk at the dinner table for the third time in one night, when your oldest son has borrowed the tool you desperately need and did not put it back where it belongs.

It happens when your authority is questioned, your will is challenged, and your plans are obstructed. Power or love. Force or influence. In the home, the choice is master or parent. On the job, the decision is boss or leader. Jesus chose to love and to lead. He knew that wielding a weapon could pierce the flesh but that washing feet would open up the soul.

Jesus was so convinced of the power of love that he said, "If someone strikes you on the right cheek, turn to him the other also. And if someone wants to sue you and take your tunic, let him have your cloak as well. If someone forces you to go one mile, go with him two miles" (Matt. 5:39–41). Paul was so convinced of the power of love that he said, "Do not be overcome by evil, but overcome evil with good" (Rom. 12:21), and love conquers all (1 Cor. 13)!

PRAYING FOR POWER

Paul prayed the Christians he discipled would receive power, and he also made it clear there was a purpose for that power:

> I pray that out of his glorious riches [God] may strengthen you with *power* through his Spirit in your inner being, so that Christ may dwell in your hearts through faith. And I pray that you, being rooted and established in love, may have *power*, together with all the Lord's holy people, to grasp how wide

and long and high and deep is the love of Christ, and to know this love that surpasses knowledge—that you may be filled to the measure of all the fullness of God. (Eph. 3:16–19, emphasis mine)

At the cross, Christ confronted his enemies not with force or with the power that was at his disposal but with his incomparable love. Suspended between two thieves, Love overcame power on the cross. History's record would from then on show that love is greater than power and ultimately will triumph over it. The resurrection is evidence that love is greater than all the power that man and Satan together can muster. In the truest sense of the word it proves power cannot keep love down.

All I can say to that is, "Thank you, Jesus."

And oh yes, "Thank you, George."

Remember... in the Seventy, we find *the love of power* will harm you but *the power of Love* will free you.

20

We Can Work It Out

It is God who works in you.

—PHILIPPIANS 2:13

You could learn something from a cheeseburger. One of my first and favorite stops whenever I am in California is the famed In-N-Out Burger. The menu is super simple, the service is fast, and the food is always good. But most of all, the name is a stroke of genius.

It seems a lot of fast-food restaurants today have gotten slower and slower in their service, or maybe my fast-world or fast-company expectations have increased. Either way, what I love about the In-N-Out Burger is that the good foods prepared *in* those places can so smoothly and quickly be picked up and taken *out* by a hungry customer like me.

In and out? Sheer genius.

Hmmm. As simple as it may sound, there is also an

in-and-out dynamic to our serving God and others in his name. To start with, people ask three huge questions about God. They are asking them all over the world right now and all around you and your world.

1. Is there a God?
2. If so, where is he?
3. And what is he doing right now?

In his letter to the Philippian church, the apostle Paul answered each of these questions. The person who wants to grow closer to Christ and to help others do the same will pay close attention to his answers. See if you can hear them in his words:

> My dear friends, as you have always obeyed—not only in my presence, but now much more in my absence—continue to work out your salvation with fear and trembling, for *it is God who works in you to will and to act according to his good purpose.*
>
> Do everything without complaining or arguing, so that you may become blameless and pure, children of God without fault in a crooked and depraved generation, in which you shine like stars in the universe as you hold out the word of life—in order that I may boast on the day of Christ that I did not run or labor for nothing.
>
> But even if I am being poured out like a drink offering on the sacrifice and service coming from your faith, I am glad and rejoice with all of you. So you too should be glad and rejoice with me. (Phil. 2:12–18, emphasis mine)

THREE ANSWERS

Did you spot the answers to the three questions? In fact, ultimately Paul also dealt with a fourth question that reveals much about how God works in our lives. And he added a fourth response to explain a bit further. Here is what Paul said that applies to your life and mine. Read these thoughtfully and carefully:

1. God is *working* ("it is God *who works*").
2. God is working *in you* ("it is God who works *in you*").[1]
3. God's will is being *worked in you* ("it is God who works in you *to will*").
4. God's will is working its way out of you ("it is God who works in you to will and to act *according to his good purpose*").

We can often overly focus on and worry about making sure we find the will of God in our lives. I like what Oswald Chambers said about this:

Being so intimately in touch with God . . . you never even need to ask Him to show you His will. It is evidence of a level of intimacy which confirms that you are nearing the final stage of your discipline in the life of faith. When you have a right-standing relationship with God, you have a life of freedom, liberty, and delight; *you are God's will*. And all your commonsense decisions are actually His will for you, unless you sense a feeling of restraint brought on by a check in your spirit. You are free to make decisions in the light of a perfect and delightful friendship with God, knowing that if your decisions are wrong He will lovingly produce that sense of restraint. Once He does, you must stop immediately.[2]

Paul taught that the will of God is not just a plan or design of God for your life; it is a power at work within you right now.

It is something he has put in you that wants to get out of you and serve others! A vital question each of us faces in the in-and-out process of growing in Christ is this: How do we work *out* what God has worked *in*?

WORKING *OUT* WHAT GOD HAS WORKED *IN* INVOLVES . . .

A Growing Obedience to the Call of God

"My dear friends, as you have always obeyed—not only in my presence, but now much more in my absence" (v. 12). Working out God's will in our lives and obedience is not above and beyond the duty of Christ followers. It is normal behavior for those of us determined to follow Christ.

A Deeper Sense of the Fear of God

"Continue to work out your salvation with fear and trembling" (v. 12). Yes, God is love, and he wants us to walk with him in that love, but he is also "a consuming fire" (Heb. 12:29 KJV). It is good for us to have a healthy sense of the fear of God, to deeply respect him and not want to disappoint him.

A Clearer Recognition of the Work of God

"For it is God who works in you to will and to act according to his good purpose" (Phil. 2:13). In the Seventy, we move from a tasting faith to a serving faith; from receiving from God to giving to others on his behalf.

Obedience is often deeply challenging. Sometimes it brings us to the end of ourselves, which is a good, but tough, place to be. C. S. Lewis said, "We shall then first be true persons when we have suffered ourselves to be fitted into our places."[3]

The Christian life is a struggle, a journey, a challenge. You can hear that in these verses, can't you?

> Run [the race] to win! (1 Cor. 9:24 NLT)
> I fight: not as one who beats the air. (1 Cor. 9:26 NKJV)
> Striving according to His working which works in me mightily. (Col. 1:29 NKJV)
> I press toward the mark for the prize of the high calling of God. (Phil. 3:14 KJV)
> Give diligence to make your calling and election sure. (2 Peter 1:10 KJV)

WORK IT OUT

When the Bible talks about our working out the will of God in our lives, the word used for "working out" is the same Greek term used for working a field or a mine. In other words, as a farmer works a field, it produces crops; as a miner works a mine, it brings forth valuable natural resources. In the same way, a scriptwriter produces a screenplay, but it takes a determined director to see the film created. A composer writes a fine musical composition, but it requires a skilled and practiced musician to make the music come to life. God has put his will within us; we are called to work it out, or, we might say, play it out.

When I go to California, almost as quickly as I drive in to my favorite local restaurant, I can drive out with just what I came for—a bag full of burgers. But just how long does it take us to work out what God has placed into our hearts and souls? What is God working in you? What challenges, opportunities, and desires is he birthing? And how well are you working out what God has already worked in your life?

Remember . . . in the Seventy, we must work
out what God has already worked in.

21

If You've Seen Me

Jesus had one supreme concern during his
earthly ministry: to glorify his Father.[1]

—David Watson

One of the most shocking moments in cinematic history came in *The Empire Strikes Back*, a film in the original Star Wars trilogy. (*Spoiler alert*: if you haven't seen the film, you may want to skip down to the next paragraph.) After a period of training with the Jedi Master, Yoda, Luke Skywalker travels to Cloud City to confront his archnemesis Darth Vader, who supposedly has killed Luke's father. During their famous light saber duel, Vader reveals he has not killed Luke's father; but, that he in fact *is* Luke's father.

I still remember the first time I saw that scene. What a shock it was to hear those words, the last plot twist I would have ever expected. It took me completely by surprise, but it wound the

131

plot springs of the epic even tighter. I never imagined Luke would have such a father, did you?

"Show Us the Father"

A similar moment occurred in the Gospels. After the Twelve had spent so much time, three years likely, with Jesus, they almost missed what was most important. In the discussion during the Last Supper, Jesus took time to shine the spotlight on two persons, the Father and the Holy Spirit. He started with the Father: "I am the way and the truth and the life. No one comes to the Father except through me. If you really know me, you will know my Father as well. From now on, you do know him and have seen him" (John 14:6–7).

Immediately Philip spoke up with a request: "Lord, show us the Father and that will be enough for us" (v. 8).

Jesus' response was likely as unexpected as Darth Vader's: "Whoever has seen me has seen the Father" (v. 9 ESV). In other words, he was saying that all this time, through all these situations and in every moment, you have not just seen me, Jesus, the Son of God. You have seen the Father God living in me and working through me. He has been revealing himself through me. Jesus even said, "I and the Father are one" (John 10:30).

Once Jesus set the Seventy straight on the real reason for rejoicing, he started to do some rejoicing of his own:

> In that same hour *he rejoiced in the Holy Spirit* and said, "I thank you, Father, Lord of heaven and earth, that you have hidden these things from the wise and understanding and revealed them to little children; yes, Father, for such was your gracious will. All things have been handed over to me by my Father, and no one knows who the Son is except the Father, or who the

Father is except the Son and anyone to whom the Son chooses to reveal him." (Luke 10:21–22 ESV, emphasis mine)

Some not-to-be-missed insights came from these words of Christ. Here are a few:

Jesus knew that many around him who seemed to be "wise and understanding" still could not see the Father. Many today may say they are Christians or that they follow Christ, but the basic question is, have they yet seen who he really is? Have their eyes been opened to see that Jesus is the only begotten Son of God? Can they see the Father and his love? Can you?

Jesus lived his life on earth to reveal the Father to those who had eyes to see. Those whose eyes God had opened were given an eyeful; that is certain. It is unfortunate but true that some people can work themselves silly for a cause and never really get to know the person for whom the cause began. Have your eyes been opened to that?

In his seminal book *Knowing God*, J. I. Packer wrote, "You sum up the whole of New Testament teaching in a single phrase, if you speak of it as a revelation of the Fatherhood of the holy Creator. . . . 'Father' is the Christian name for God."[2]

Jesus was given the authority to reveal the Father to people on earth. "No one knows who the Son is except the Father, or who the Father is except the Son and anyone to whom the Son chooses to reveal him" (v. 22 ESV). The gospel is not only a story that shows us how to get to heaven one day; it is the power of God that brings us into the heavenly Father's embrace right now!

Jesus lived his life on earth to show his followers how to live in a loving relationship with their heavenly Father. Regardless of the kind of relationship you have had with your earthly father, Jesus came to give you a relationship with your Father in heaven that is like none other. Jesus is not only a great Savior for you and me; he was and is a great Son. In like manner, you and I are called to live our lives embracing the identity of sons and daughters of God. Dallas Willard observed, "Genuine transformation of the whole person into the goodness and power seen in Jesus and his 'Abba' Father . . . remains the necessary goal of human life."[3]

Jesus wanted to bring his followers into the joy that is the Trinity. The God of the Bible is not an isolated potentate but a fellowship of persons, the Three—Father, Son, and Holy Spirit. Among these Three there continues to be an interactive union like none other. Jesus thought so much of it that when he prayed for his followers, he prayed to the Father "that they [that is, you and me, his followers] will all be one, just as you and I [that is, Jesus and his Father] are one" (John 17:21 NLT).

Jesus the Son lived his life on earth as a part of a dynamic fellowship of persons called the Trinity. Jesus the Son was so connected to his Father that he constantly kept a "spotlight" on the heavenly Father: "In this instance [and others], Jesus immediately defers the honor [he receives] to his Father, shining the spotlight straightly and swiftly on him."[4] See if you can recognize all the times he does so in this passage:

> Jesus responded to the Jewish leaders, "I assure you that the Son can't do anything by himself except what he sees the Father doing. Whatever the Father does, the Son does likewise. The Father loves the Son and shows him everything that he does. He will show him greater works than these so that you will marvel. As the Father raises the dead and gives life, so too does the Son give life to whomever he wishes. The Father doesn't judge anyone, but he has given all judgment to the Son so that everyone will honor the Son just as they honor the Father. Whoever doesn't honor the Son doesn't honor the Father who sent him." (John 5:19–23 CEB)

So You Can See the Father

Dallas Willard explained the imperfect state of the circles of human relationship we experience in life and the Perfect Circle to which they all point: "Ultimately, every human circle is doomed to dissolution if it is not caught up in the life of the only genuinely self-sufficient circle of sufficiency, that of the Father, Son, and Holy Spirit. For that circle is the only one that is truly and totally self-sufficient. And all the broken circles must ultimately find their healing there."[5]

Of all the gifts and graces we experience from Jesus in the Five Thousand and the works we are enabled to do for him in the Seventy, there is more he yet wants to do in us. As we experience his blessings and engage his works, we can often long for more. It is as if our hearts say, "Lord, I don't just want to do what you are doing; I want to go where you are going. Bring me to a place where I am not just working for the Lord but more fully walking with the Lord."

David Platt wrote, "This is the heart of following Jesus: enjoying God as Father through Christ the Son. And when this is a reality in your life, then your reason for living is utterly revolutionized."[6]

Jesus came to save you from sin and yourself and to show you just how great a Father's love can truly be—in fact, a father and son so close that you can hardly tell them apart. And as a father calls his son to his side, so Jesus has a closer call for us that will demand more of us.

Are you ready to go to the places he is calling you?

The Son is calling you closer to himself, so close that you can see the Father.

Remember . . . in the Seventy, we find Jesus came not
only to save us but also to show us a perfect Father.

The Twelve

Following the Call of Christ

"When Jesus first approached me that day and said, 'Come,' I assumed he had another short assignment in mind for me. As he had done with the Seventy, perhaps he wanted me to visit another town to prepare for his coming. But, no, this call was something entirely different. First of all, it was no short-term assignment. He was calling me to leave the world of my own designs, to leave my work and vocation, and to simply 'follow.' He didn't call me to take a leave of absence; he wanted me to make a whole-life commitment. From this moment on my new job title would be a 'fisher of men,' and its one objective was what he described in two unforgettable words: 'Follow me.' "

22

The Following Leader

*Jesus wasn't looking for leaders at all.
Jesus was looking for followers.*[1]

—LEONARD SWEET

It's time to pull over for a while on this journey together and enter a rest area. Let's retrace our steps a bit and get our bearings. In our walk with Christ, we move from

> the Crowds, which represent *the places of watching and listening,* where we gain *a view of Christ* in our lives. Then we journey to
> the Five Thousand, which represent *the places of feeding and healing,* where we experience some of *the blessings of Christ.* Then we follow to
> the Seventy, which represent *the places of serving and*

working, where we enter into the *work of Christ.* Then we come to
the Twelve, which represent the places of . . .

Well, let's find out together. Consider how Jesus formed this circle of intimate allies:

> [Jesus] went up on the mountain and called to him those whom he desired, and they came to him. And he appointed twelve (whom he also named apostles) so they might be with him and he might send them out to preach and have authority to cast out demons. He appointed the twelve: Simon (to whom he gave the name Peter); James the son of Zebedee and John the brother of James (to whom he gave the name Boanerges, that is, Sons of Thunder); Andrew, and Philip, and Bartholomew, and Matthew, and Thomas, and James the son of Alphaeus, and Thaddaeus, and Simon the Zealot, and Judas Iscariot, who betrayed him. (Mark 3:13–19 ESV)

Jesus did not start his public ministry by choosing disciples. No, it appears he ministered on his own for a period of time, watching the Crowds grow around him. Then around the half-way point of his ministry, he chose the Twelve. The Scottish minister and professor A. B. Bruce described it this way:

> The selection by Jesus of the twelve . . . divides the minis-try of our Lord into two portions, nearly equal. . . . In the earlier period, Jesus labored single-handed; His miraculous deeds were confined for the most part to a limited area, and His teaching was [more] elementary. . . . But by the time when the twelve were chosen, the work of the kingdom had assumed such dimensions as to require organization and

division of labor; and the teaching of Jesus was beginning to be of a deeper and more elaborate nature.[2]

THREE THINGS

Jesus drew the Twelve closer to him for three specific reasons. First, however, notice what those reasons were not. Jesus did *not* appoint them . . .

- to be independent. No, he called them "so that they might be with him." It was a relational call.
- to be silent. No, he called them so "he might send them out to preach." From the account, it appears this preaching was almost instantaneous.
- to be powerless. No, he called them that they might "have authority to cast out demons." Jesus faced a world full of serious illnesses, issues, and bondages. The disciples were clothed with the power of Christ.

But note that Jesus did not overly focus on leadership, not the way some pastors and teachers do today. I cannot find one place in all his red-letter words where Jesus called any man to lead, to be a leader, or to leadership.

If the key word within the influence of Jesus' passion and persona was not *lead, led, leader,* or *leadership,* what was it?

Follow.

He repeated the word many times:

"Come, follow me." (Matt. 4:19)

"Follow Me, and I will make you fishers of men." (Matt. 4:19 NASB)

"One thing you lack. . . . Go, sell everything you have and give to the poor, and you will have treasure in heaven.

Then come, follow me." (Mark 10:21)

"My sheep listen to my voice; I know them, and they follow
me." (John 10:27)

"Whoever serves me must follow me; and where I am, my
servant also will be." (John 12:26)

Leonard Sweet summed it up well: "We have been told our
entire lives that we should be leaders, that we need more leaders,
leaders, leaders. But the truth is that the greatest way to create a movement is to be a follower and to show others how to
follow. Following is the most underrated form of leadership in
existence."[3]

At this point in the journey of the Christ follower, in the
place of the Twelve, we have received the words and gifts of
Christ and enjoyed his blessings, and we now feel compelled
to join him in his journey of faith. We are drawn to Jesus' journey. And with that drawing toward his path, our motivation is
belonging to Christ. At this place, what matters most is no longer what he does for us but only that he walks with us.

MY JOURNEY INTO THE TWELVE

No, I am not one of the twelve apostles of Jesus, but I *am* called
to be his disciple, his follower. For me, I believe the sense of this
calling or what I describe as coming into the place of the Twelve
from Jesus came during my first couple of years as a Christ follower. The experience of reading the Bible, drawing closer to
God in prayer, and engaging in meaningful community and fellowship with other Christ followers just did something to me
and within me. It changed me deeply.

John said it this way: "If we walk in the light, as [Jesus] is in
the light, we have fellowship with one another, and the blood of
Jesus, his Son, purifies us from all sin" (1 John 1:7). That process

describes my experience. Along with it, however, came a growing and deeper sense that God was calling me to leave some things in my life and replace them with new things. Your experience of coming into the place of the Twelve may have been (or may yet be) quite different from mine. I sensed God calling me to do the following:

- Leave my own plans for my future, and follow his plans, whatever they may be.
- Leave the people and practices in my life that were drawing me away from God, and follow those that would bring me closer to him.
- Leave the fears that were holding me back in my walk with Christ, and follow in the bolder steps toward which faith was calling me.

The call to follow Jesus changed my primary passions and pursuits. Finding out more and more about Jesus, his words, his ways, and his will became my preoccupation. Following him meant leaving other things behind.

"Follow Me"

When Jesus said, "Follow me," he called the disciples to leave everything and follow him. They left their lives as they had known them, their vocations, their homes, their comforts, and their comforting friends, just to follow Jesus and to be a part of whatever he was up to. So when we come to the Twelve, this represents *the places of leaving all and following* Jesus. Have you stepped into that circle in your faith walk? If so, what has Christ called you to leave, and how has he called you to follow? Did you leave? Are you following?

Even after crisscrossing the globe with the gospel and

setting flames of devotion among the Gentiles and in the corridors of kings, the apostle Paul communicated his call to leadership this way: "Follow my example, as I follow the example of Christ" (1 Cor. 11:1).

The call of Christ is first and foremost a call to follow. The true test of leadership is determined by how effective we are at helping others follow well. What the world needs more right now than another leadership conference or book is one man or woman determined to follow Christ better and to help others do the same.

We tend to focus on the *leaders* and the *leadership*.

Jesus focuses on the *following*.

What about you?

Do you follow?

Remember . . . in the Twelve, we follow
Jesus to the places of leaving all.

23

Let's Get This Show on the Road

*You can't become famous if you hide like this! If you can
do such wonderful things, show yourself to the world!*

—John 7:4 NLT

Many remember a time when Jesus stood silent before his
accusers, but there was another time, much less remembered,
when he shouted out loud. He raised his voice above the fes-
tal crowd, and for a moment on this side of heaven, the Lion of
Judah roared.

Things were heating up in Jesus' ministry just before this
shouting occurred—miracles, healings, teaching with unprecedented authority, and more. The lines were being drawn,
however. Decisions were being made. His brothers gave him
advice. In order to gain more followers, they urged him to move
from the more remote regions of Galilee and to take the road
show to Judea in order to do public relations work. "No one

who wants to become a public figure acts in secret," they told him. "Since you are doing these [miracles], show yourself to the world" (John 7:4). In other words, they were telling Jesus: "Now is your time. Seize the opportunity! Make hay while the sun and the spotlights shine."

The Message offers Jesus' response: "Jesus came back at them, 'Don't *crowd* me. This isn't my time. It's your time—it's *always* your time; you have nothing to lose. The world has nothing against you, but it's up in arms against me. It's against me because I expose the evil behind its pretensions. You go ahead, go up to the Feast. Don't wait for me. I'm not ready. It's not the right time for me" (vv. 6–8, emphasis mine).

Jesus was not about to follow their counsel. His ways were unlike theirs. Pastor Zack Eswine stated, "Jesus would have driven any publicist and congregation mad. After he would do something great [such as healing someone], he often asked that no one say anything about it."[1]

His brothers went on to Jerusalem, but Jesus chose to stay in Galilee. Not long afterward, Jesus journeyed on his own to the Holy City, "not publicly, but in secret" (v. 10). A feast was being celebrated, and the city was abuzz with controversy. Everyone wanted to know, "Where is that man?" He was the talk of the town.

THE GREAT OUTPOURING

Ultimately on his own timetable and amid the annual feast, Jesus showed up. Everyone wondered whether he would come to the city. He did, and he went right to the middle of the temple courts and began teaching. Many were amazed at his authority, his teaching, and his insight. The Jews asked, "How did this man get such learning without having studied?" (v. 15).

Jesus responded readily:

"My teaching is not my own. It comes from him who sent me. If anyone chooses to do God's will, he will find out whether my teaching comes from God or whether I speak on my own. He who speaks on his own does so to gain honor for himself, but he who works for the honor of the one who sent him is a man of truth; there is nothing false about him." (vv. 16–18)

The atmosphere tensing by the moment, the Man of Truth confronted his critics even more clearly as the day went on: "Has not Moses given you the law? Yet not one of you keeps the law. Why are you trying to kill me?" (v. 19).

To appreciate the power and significance of what Jesus said and did that day, we need to consider a little more background of the event going on in Jerusalem, the Feast of Tabernacles. This major celebration on Israel's worship calendar took place about six months before the crucifixion of Christ that year. The annual autumn feast was designed to commemorate Israel's forty-year journey through the wilderness. The last day in particular climaxed the week of celebration. Tents and little shelters were built from branches to house families in order to remember God's leadership of their ancestors through the wilderness with Moses.

Tradition tells us of a climactic event called the "great water-pouring" ceremony, which was a part of this week of celebrations. At a specific time, the priests took huge urns filled with water and simultaneously poured them from atop the temple steps. Just picture it. Gallons and gallons of water beautifully cascaded out of the temple, down the steps, and toward the people, creating a waterfall at their place of worship. Remembering the significance of water provisions in the barren wilderness brought added significance to this event, as hundreds of years earlier under Moses' leadership God had sent water from a rock at Meribah.

Just as the priests began to pour their urns of water with synchronistic precision from the top of the temple steps, joy would most certainly erupt among the people in shouts and praises. The drama ran high as the Israelites lifted up praises to God as they remembered his faithfulness.

The combination of bold vocal praise to God and the river-like flow of water from the temple was so significant that Jesus thought it was an opportunity too good to miss. Just as the eruption of the people's response started to calm, Jesus shouted. The word used here (Greek, *krazo*)[2] indicates an alarming shout, an exclamation, a virtual scream of excitement. Jesus raised his voice high and passionately above the crowd: "On the last and greatest day of the Feast, Jesus stood and said in a loud voice, 'If anyone is thirsty, let him come to me and drink. Whoever believes in me, as the Scripture has said, streams of living water will flow from within him'" (vv. 37–38).

As the water cascaded down from the top steps of the house of worship and poured step over step until it covered some of the sandals of the onlookers, the Lord saw something exhilarating on the prophetic horizon. He envisioned a time when not just *one* temple of stone but millions and millions of spiritual temples all over the world would be endued with the Spirit of God to the point of an overflow in their lives. Out of their very spirits ("innermost beings") a current would come, and out would pour "rivers of living water" (v. 38 KJV). Such an inspired thought in the mind of Christ refused to be merely whispered or merely contemplated; it insisted on being shouted out loud.

Experience the Difference

No religious leaders asked Jesus to take part in the ceremony that day. He had not been commissioned by any man to do so. His name was not on the order of worship written out by the scribes and Pharisees. He did not ask anyone for permission to speak. He powerfully lifted his voice uninvited and unannounced. He was on heaven's agenda that day. The announcement was his to make. It erupted; it poured forth. Just as John the Baptist heralded the coming of the Messiah in the wilderness bold and unhindered, so now Jesus was heralding the coming of the Spirit in a most liberated and authoritative manner.

Christ had come *to* their town; soon the Spirit would pour *from* their lives.

Remember... in the Twelve, as we believe in God's Son, his Spirit pours through our lives like rivers.

24

The Gospel According to Peter?

*The gospel is not about choosing to follow
advice, it's about choosing to follow a King.*[1]

—TIMOTHY KELLER

Some things are best left unsaid; others, unwritten. In 1886, a
French archaeologist recovered an ancient document called
the Gospel According to Peter. It turned out to be one of the
early supposed records of the life and ministry of Jesus that was
considered when the books of the Bible were compiled into the
canon of Scripture. However, Peter's purported gospel did not
make the cut. For numerous reasons, the early church fathers
did not accept it as either authentic or reliable.

Still, I wonder. Had Peter actually penned a gospel, what
would he have included, and what would he have left out? One
of the most difficult stories for him to include may have also

been one of his most affirming moments, the visit to Caesarea Philippi with Jesus and the Twelve.

As Jesus and his disciples arrived that day in the district of Caesarea Philippi, an ancient Roman city located near the base of Mount Hermon, Jesus seemed interested to hear a bit more about the buzz among the people. He wanted to discuss what they were hearing and what people were saying on the streets. Jesus asked the disciples, "Who do people say the Son of Man is?" (Matt. 16:13).

By then much water had flowed under the bridge of Jesus' ministry. Parables taught. Blind eyes healed. Sermons preached. Disciples assembled. Miracles performed. Something now, however, was brewing in the atmosphere—a sea change was afoot. Jesus' question would prove to be more of a test than a conversational tool.

The disciples cited at least a few answers to Christ's question. It seems the Crowds couldn't quite make up their minds about who Jesus was. But they had a few ideas: "Some say John the Baptist; others say Elijah; and still others, Jeremiah or one of the prophets" (v. 14).

JESUS' OTHER QUESTION

But Jesus had another question. While his first one painted a broad swath of curiosity, his second one was penetratingly personal. He said to them, "Who do *you* say I am?" (v. 15, emphasis mine). Although the Greek word here for "you," *hymeis*, is plural, implying Jesus was asking all the disciples, I believe Jesus looked straight at Peter when he asked the question. If he did not, it certainly appears the question struck Peter in such a way that he answered immediately, whether for himself or the entire group. Then again, he was an assertive one, wasn't he?

Simon Peter replied, "You are the Christ, the Son of the

living God" (v. 16 ESV). I think everyone froze when Peter spoke those words. It was an amazing and pivotal moment in Christ's ministry. I call it Jesus' Eureka moment! *Eureka* is an expression dating back to the ancient scientist and mathematician Archimedes. He used it with exhilarating excitement to celebrate a new discovery, one he had long sought. It means an enthusiastic "I found it!"

When Peter said, "You are the Christ," he was saying something no one else had yet said about Jesus. The Crowds spoke of Jesus' identity as speculation, but Peter did so by revelation. Here's how Jesus celebrated the moment: He said to Peter, "Blessed are you, Simon Bar-Jonah! For flesh and blood has not revealed this to you, but my Father who is in heaven. And I tell you, you are Peter, and on this rock I will build my church, and the gates of hell shall not prevail against it. I will give you the keys of the kingdom of heaven, and whatever you bind on earth shall be bound in heaven, and whatever you loose on earth shall be loosed in heaven" (vv. 17–19 ESV).

What an astounding set of promises and powers Christ conferred on Peter in this moment! Take another look at them. He told Peter, and I paraphrase:

"You are blessed!"
"No mere human being revealed this to you."
"God the Father is speaking to you, Peter!"
"Your bold faith has made you like a rock!"
"The church I am building is unstoppable; not even hell itself can stop it!"
"Because of your bold faith, I am giving you the authority to unleash heaven on earth, to bring God's work into the lives of people. In fact, here are the keys. Let's get it started."

Talk about affirmations. As one of the Twelve, Peter was stepping up to the question Jesus had just asked. Not only was

Christ's question eventful; so was Peter's answer. Affirmations like those go either to your heart or to your head; just a few short moments, and we would find out.

CHRIST'S CONFIDANT

Not only did Peter's confession draw strong words of affirmation from Christ; they also informed him that now was the time to move to a new level of forthrightness with his disciples: "*From that time* Jesus began to show his disciples that he must go to Jerusalem and suffer many things from the elders and chief priests and scribes, and be killed, and on the third day be raised" (v. 21 ESV, emphasis mine).

WHAT WE WANT TO HEAR

To say Peter didn't really like this next lesson of Jesus' discipleship course would be quite the understatement. Check this out: "Peter took him aside and began to rebuke him, saying, 'Far be it from you, Lord! This shall never happen to you'" (v. 22 ESV). Yes, you read that right. Peter rebuked Jesus.

Ironically Peter's contemporaries would likely have judged him as the most unruly of Jesus' disciples, the most prone toward rugged independence, and yet Jesus ultimately set him up as the leader (or lead follower) of his church. Apparently what we regard as roughshod and rebellious, Jesus considered raw material for a leader in the making. The beloved Scottish biographer of biblical characters, Alexander Whyte, said of Peter: "These are Peter's unmistakable footprints. Hasty, headlong, speaking impertinently and unadvisedly, ready to repent, ever wading into waters too deep for him, and ever turning to his Master again like a little child."[2]

REBUKING JESUS?

Within moments, it seemed, of boldly affirming Jesus' messiahship on the streets of Casearea, Peter turned the tables on him. The confrontations started to fly. Author and New York City pastor Tim Keller wrote, "Peter begins to 'rebuke' [Jesus]. This is the verb used elsewhere for what Jesus does to demons. This means Peter is condemning Jesus in the strongest possible language. Why is Peter so undone, that he would turn on Jesus like this right after identifying him as the Messiah?"[3]

Jesus' famous response to Peter's resistance was a rebuke: "Get behind me, Satan!" (v. 23 ESV). In this scathing rebuke, Jesus was saying Peter was an offense. Much as Satan had tried to tempt Jesus in the wilderness, now "Jesus was rebuking Peter for being a hindrance to His mission, for offering Him a tantalizing way out of His deadly mission that would prove to be a trap."[4]

Fortunately this disciple's journey did not end there. In order for Peter to get to the next level in his walk with Christ, he needed a serious confrontation. In fact, he required several in his life. On the heels of his rich affirmation in Caesarea Philippi, he had suddenly copped an attitude in response to Christ that was rich on so many levels. While he waxed articulate and set Jesus straight, he didn't know he was about to be dressed down at a whole new level.

Had Peter actually written one of the four Gospels, he might have been tempted to leave out the next part of this story.

Remember ... in the Twelve, we find that although God
is speaking, sometimes we don't like what he has to say.

25

The Line Jesus Drew in the Sand

The disciple of Christ cannot lose: when he gives
all, he gains all; when he loses his life, he finds it.[1]

—David Watson

Ordinary is the best adjective to describe Jesus' disciples. They were not special. None among them had a list of honors on his résumé. You would not have naturally chosen them from the Crowds. There were no summa cum laudes or magna cum laudes; not even close.

John MacArthur wrote of the disciples:

> They were perfectly ordinary men in every way. Not one of them was renowned for scholarship. . . . They had no track record as orators or theologians. . . . They were not outstanding because of any natural talents or intellectual abilities. On

the contrary, they were all too prone to mistakes, misstatements, wrong attitudes, lapses of faith, and bitter failure—no one more so than the leader of the group, Peter. Even Jesus remarked that they were slow learners and somewhat spiritually dense (Luke 24:25).[2]

THE LINE

Once Jesus opened up and shared more with his followers about the challenges they would face, remember Peter corrected Jesus. Peter then proceeded to tell him there would be nothing of the sort of sufferings he predicted.

Apparently that was where Peter crossed a line with Jesus. At that strategic moment, Jesus drew a proverbial line in the sand laying out clearly to this leader in the making, Peter, exactly what the call of Christ involved and that his kind of leadership would be characterized by faithful following.

Here's how Jesus spelled it out. This was his discipleship call to the Twelve then and still is to us today: "If anyone would come after me, let him deny himself and take up his cross and follow me" (Matt. 16:24 ESV).

R. C. Sproul drove home the force of Jesus' call here: "This is one of the clearest, starkest statements of what the Christian life is about that we find in all of Scripture. To follow Christ is to live in the shadow of the cross. If we want to join Him in His glory, if we want to participate in His exaltation, first we must join Him in His disgrace, shame, and humiliation. We must be willing to die."[3] But just what is *discipleship* really? Francis Chan defined it this way: "Discipleship is a lifelong process where we are continuously made more and more like Jesus."[4]

THE CALL OF CHRIST

Let's zoom in closer on the major aspects of the call of Christ. The call of Christ is a call to follow. Christ's call is also . . . [5]

A Call to Intimacy

Jesus said, "If anyone would come after me . . ." (Matt. 16:24 ESV). The call of Christ is the call to follow him, to come closer to him, to "come after" him. Peter seemed to have had his own ideas of what Christ desired. Sometimes, so do we. Jesus corrected those misconceptions.

David Watson described the closeness to which Jesus calls his followers:

> The call by Jesus was also a call to Jesus. [New disciples in these times were expected] to commit themselves to a specific teaching or cause. But the call of Jesus was personal: he called his disciples to follow him, to be with him, and to commit themselves wholeheartedly to him. They could become disciples only by repenting of their sin and by believing in him.
>
> When Jesus called individuals to be his disciples, he shared his life with them. By his incarnation he identified himself fully with them, and he made himself vulnerable by opening his heart to them. Part of his great attraction lay in the fact that his love was so real and open that others sensed intuitively that they could trust him. . . . His transparent openness and integrity drew others into a quality of loving that they had not known before.[6]

A Call to Humility

Jesus said, "You must forget about yourself" (Matt. 16:24 CEV). The follower of Christ is called to "deny himself" (ESV).

159

The call of Christ is not primarily a call to self-fulfillment but more one of self-denial and self-surrender.

C. S. Lewis wrote:

> The more we get what we now call "ourselves" out of the way and let Him take us over, the more truly ourselves we become. . . . [Our] real selves are all waiting for us in Him. . . . The more I resist Him and try to live on my own, the more I become dominated by my own heredity and upbringing and surroundings and natural desires. . . . What I call "My wishes" become merely the desires thrown up by my physical organism or pumped into me by other men's thoughts. . . . It is when I turn to Christ, when I give myself up to His Personality, that I first begin to have a real personality of my own.[7]

A Call to Serenity

Jesus said, "You must . . . take up your cross" (Matt. 16:24 NLT). Christ had a cross to bear, and he tells us to expect the same. Our crosses represent not only the challenges, struggles, and hardships God allows in our lives but also the attitudes we maintain amid those struggles. Instead of letting our crosses bring us down, we must take them up and move forward in Christ. The call to serenity is a call to accept not only the blessings of God but also the challenges of life through his grace. Instead of denying, resisting, or resenting the crosses we face, we are to instead "take up" each one with a deep trust in the one who carried his cross so well.

A Call to Loyalty

Jesus said, "You must . . . follow me" (Matt. 16:24 NLT). Peter had his own ideas of what following Christ would look like and require. It appeared he wanted a certain kind of Jesus, one of his own wishes or designs. A preferred Jesus, you might say. Perhaps Peter wanted more of a Christ who would bring him comforts and prestige, rather than one who would allow him to face challenges. Despite that, Jesus laid out in no uncertain terms that obedience involved following with the utmost loyalty.

In an age of mass-marketing appeal, we too often try to water down and sanitize the rough and difficult dynamics of Christ's call. R. C. Sproul commented, "When we seek to win converts to Christianity, we often do everything we can to persuade them of all the benefits they will receive if they will give their lives to Jesus."[8] Jesus wasn't concerned about marketing for consumers; he was drawing a clear line in the sand for all who would be his devoted followers.

EVERYTHING ELSE SECOND

Jesus took this golden opportunity to unpack what he meant about following him. He took time to let the disciples know what it meant to follow him. Tim Keller wrote,

> When Jesus says to Simon and Andrew, "Come, follow me," at once they leave their vocation as fishermen and follow him. When he calls James and John, they leave behind their father and friends, right there in the boat. We know from reading the rest of the Gospels that these men did fish again, and they did continue to relate to their parents. But what Jesus is saying is still disruptive. In traditional cultures you get your identity from your family. And so when Jesus says, "I want priority over your family," that's drastic. In our individualistic culture, on the other hand, saying good-bye to our parents isn't a big deal, but for Jesus to say, "I want priority over your career"—*that's* drastic. Jesus is saying, "Knowing me, loving me, resembling me, serving me must

become the supreme passion of your life. Everything else comes second."[9]

Peter had preconceived notions about the call of Christ, and so do we. But the same hands that were nail pierced because of love drew an unflinching line in the sand to make clear his call to Peter, to the rest of the Twelve, and to you.

And there is nothing ordinary about that.

Remember... in the Twelve, ordinary people receive an extraordinary call from Christ.

26

The Power of A.S.K.

Everyone who asks receives.

—Luke 11:10

When I pastored a church in the Boston area, one of our favorite family vacation spots in the summer was Wells, Maine. The rocky cliffs and shoals, the shorelines and quaint beach cottages, and the fantastic seafood shacks made it a fun spot for us to get away.

One of our rituals was to drop by the local bakery and coffee shop in the morning, pick up snacks, and then look for a scenic spot to have a time of family devotions, which usually included a Bible passage or story and a time of prayer. One year when our two oldest daughters were about twelve and fourteen, we decided to ask them to take turns leading the devotions and prayer time. I thought it might be fun and interesting to hear how a twelve-year-old would teach the Bible.

Our devotional focus for the week was to read through

the Sermon on the Mount. This particular morning our energetic and enthusiastic second-born, Kara Joy, was up. She read over her passage, which was a familiar one Jesus taught to his disciples:

> Ask, and it will be given to you; seek, and you will find; knock, and it will be opened to you. For everyone who asks receives, and the one who seeks finds, and to the one who knocks it will be opened. Or which one of you, if his son asks him for bread, will give him a stone? Or if he asks for a fish, will give him a serpent? If you then, who are evil, know how to give good gifts to your children, how much more will your Father who is in heaven give good things to those who ask him! (Matt. 7:7–11 ESV)

Too Cute

Listening to my daughter read the Word of God in the beautiful ocean setting with the waves providing a soothing rhythmic score, I thought: *Oh, isn't she cute. I have taught and preached on this passage so many times over the years, let's see what her young little mind does with the passage. If she stumbles, I may have to help her along a bit on the interpretation and application points.*

I will never forget the simple way Kara described this passage. "When I first read this," Kara said, "I thought, *I have heard it a lot of times before.* I know Jesus was talking about prayer, but what I thought was cool were the three words he used for it: *ask, seek,* and *knock.* After reading over it a few times and praying, I realized each one of these three steps requires something more from me. Asking is something you can do while sitting down. But seeking means you have to get up and move around a bit and look. You have to use your feet with your faith. Then with knocking it requires even more commitment. You have to put yourself into knocking. You have to get up, move somewhere, and use your body. Knock, knock, knock. I think Jesus was telling his disciples not just to pray or to pray harder but to pray with everything in them, *everything*, even with their whole hearts."

The next thing I remember saying was nothing at all. I was stunned by the simplicity, the clarity, and the penetrating accuracy of a little girl who took Jesus at his word, at face value. And although I had heard and read countless treatments of this passage before and have read several commentaries since, I have never heard an explanation of it I have found any more convicting, practical, and applicable than this one.

One of the most important practices of a Christ follower and a disciple of Jesus is *asking*. On one occasion Jesus said to the Twelve, "Until now you have not asked for anything in my name. Ask and you will receive, and your joy will be complete" (John 16:24). Jesus said this during some of his final words on earth and just before he broke into what is famously known as his High Priestly Prayer (John 17). The disciples were unlike the mother of James and John, who eagerly approached Jesus and made a bold request. Jesus was correcting his disciples and letting them know they were missing a golden opportunity when they didn't ask. Imagine having Jesus spend a day with you, he with all the power and authority of heaven, and yet you do not ask him a thing.

Ask and you *will* receive.
Seek and you *will* find.
Knock and the door *will* be open.

Prayer is whatever place we find to draw close to God, to be intimate with him, and to practice being in his presence. But as a part of that intimate journey, he invites us to ask. In fact, the tone of the Matthew 7 passage on ask-seek-knock is more of an imperative or a command.

DINNER WITH AN AUTHOR

Years ago I had the rare opportunity to have lunch with one of my favorite Christian authors. I wanted to ask him several questions. Already sensing a deep desire to write more at that stage in my life, I thought, *What a great opportunity. I am sitting with one of the most respected authors in the world. This is no time to be bashful. It's time to ask up!*

"Gary, how did you come upon the opportunity to write and publish books? What was your first break?"

"My prayer closet," Gary said without hesitation.

"Oh yes, right," I responded. "I'm sure you have prayed about this a lot. But what I mean is, what brought about the first book? Did you know someone in the publishing industry?"

"No. Honestly, it all started with my prayer time."

"Tell me more," I asked, intrigued at his point and his passion.

"Well, as I pray in the mornings, I have a habit of practicing ask-seek-knock. The more I prayed, the more I felt the passion to write. This experience more and more convinced me that writing was not just something I wanted, but something God wanted me to do. So, I just kept praying and asking. Before too long, God put some ideas in my heart about ways to seek and knock related to this desire. But the desire, the passion, and the direction really came from my prayer closet."

As Gary, an experienced and published author, shared these insights with me, I could picture it. In my mind's eye, I could see him sitting on the floor of his living room early in the morning with his Bible opened and bringing his passions and desires to God in prayer. Asking, asking more, and asking again. As he did, the passion became stronger, clearer, and more focused.

I have found that the ask-seek-knock insight Jesus gave his disciples is a powerful one. Since then, I have seen God use this as a passion filter in my life that repeatedly teaches me to let go of my will and take hold of his.

When it comes to asking in prayer, God invites us to do so. When it comes to how, I think Gary had it right, and so did twelve-year-old Kara. So, that means Jesus calls us to not only follow closely but also ask boldly!

Remember... in the Twelve, we find that following Christ faithfully involves asking him boldly.

27

Get Your Joy On

*Jesus promised his disciples three things—
that they would be completely fearless,
absurdly happy, and in constant trouble.*[1]

—F. R. MALTBY

Jesus wants his followers to experience great joy. I am convinced of this. As late as his Last Supper discourse, he let them know they could find joy in part from their prayer life: "Until now you have asked nothing in my name. Ask, and you will receive, that your joy may be full" (John 16:24 ESV).

I know Christians are *supposed* to be joyful people. And I realize joy is a result of having the Spirit in me. Among all the people of the earth, Christians have the greatest reason to be full of joy. But sometimes life steps in and robs me of the joy. I know I should feel it, but sometimes I just don't. The questions emerge: *Is joy something I should just wait for? Will it just come upon me?*

169

I am not alone. There seems to be a great absence of joy in the lives of many Christians and congregations today. Of the several fruits "of the Spirit" (Gal. 5:22–23), joy seems to be the most elusive.

Interestingly enough, the Bible never *recommends* we rejoice; it *commands* us to do so ("I will say it again: Rejoice!" [Phil. 4:4]). When I first realized this, a few questions immediately came to mind: *How can I suddenly have the emotion of joy? According to the Bible, how can it be cultivated? In short, what can I do to work on my joy?*

After plowing through some of these questions, I made up my mind a few years ago that I wanted to be a joyful Christian, not periodically, but consistently. I wanted to be a person who regularly experiences the fullness of joy that Christ promised. Most of all, I wanted my experience and expression to be authentic, real, and contagious.

But God won't force the expression of joy on us. Much like a host throwing a party, who invites you to the event in full hopes you will absolutely enjoy yourself, he provides all that is needed for a good time—the atmosphere, the food, the people—but your attitude and actions determine how much you enjoy the event.

DISCIPLINES LEADING TO JOY

In order to tap into the joy supply Christ has secured for us, we will need discipline. Joy is not merely an emotion felt within; it is a discipline we must cultivate and practice. The Bible makes it clear that certain disciplines in our daily routine will lead to a greater sense of joy. Here are some I have found:

1. Joy Reads!

Reading the Scripture can be an incredible source of joy. The psalmist apparently tapped into this source of joy often: "The commandments of the LORD are right, bringing joy to the heart"

(Ps. 19:8 NLT), and "I rejoice in your word like one who discovers a great treasure" (Ps. 119:162 NLT).

2. Joy Sings!

Singing, whether in a church or in my car, is one of my favorite ways to stir up and release the joy of the Lord in my heart. Singing allows my soul to move its focus away from the circumstances of life and toward the character of God. It's downright therapeutic. Even Paul encouraged the Ephesian Christians to make music a habit in their lives: "Be filled with the Spirit.... Sing and make music from your heart to the Lord" (Eph. 5:18–19).

3. Joy Gives!

A generous spirit is a joyous spirit. Paul praised the Corinthians for their cheerful giving: "Now I want you to know, dear brothers and sisters, what God in his kindness has done through the churches in Macedonia. They are being tested by many troubles, and they are very poor. But they are also filled with abundant joy, which has overflowed in rich generosity" (2 Cor. 8:1–2 NLT).

4. Joy Communes!

At this stage of growth in Christ, in the Twelve, the primary characteristic of a follower is being a comrade. Our focus and much of our joy come not only from walking with Christ, or working for Christ but also from doing both of these together with others in community. "How good and pleasant it is when brothers live together in unity! ... For there the LORD bestows his blessing, even life forevermore" (Ps. 133:1, 3).

5. Joy Meditates!

Our joy is renewed by remembering God, by meditating on his goodness, by recalling his specific acts of faithfulness to us:

> *You satisfy me more than the richest feast.*
>   *I will praise you with songs of joy.*
> *I lie awake thinking of you,*
>   *meditating on you through the night.*
> *Because you are my helper,*
>   *I sing for joy in the shadow of your wings.*
>   (Ps. 63:5–7 NLT)

6. Joy Serves!

Jesus came into this world presenting himself as a servant, not a king (Phil. 2). He came to show us that the greatest joy is found when we learn how to truly serve God and people in need. The journey of serving God is supposed to be one paved with great joy: "Serve the LORD with gladness" (Ps. 100:2 NKJV).

7. Joy Enjoys!

What about enjoying God? God wants us to worship him, and he wants us to *enjoy* him. The psalmist wrote, "In thy presence is fulness of joy; at thy right hand there are pleasures for evermore" (Ps. 16:11 KJV). Pastor John Piper says, "God is most glorified in us when we are most satisfied in Him."[2]

CHOOSING JOY

C. S. Lewis also recognized the importance of making the joy choice, even when doubts arose:

> Moods will change, whatever view your reason takes. I know that by experience. Now that I am a Christian I do have moods in which the whole thing [Christianity] looks very improbable: but when I was an atheist I had moods in which Christianity looked terribly probable. . . . That is why Faith is such a necessary virtue: *unless you teach your moods "where*

they get off," you can never be either a sound Christian or even a sound atheist.[3]

In the final analysis, joy is a regular experience no Christian can afford to miss. It requires certain disciplines, but they are well worth it. Growing in Christ takes us from one experience of finding our joy in God to another. Paul referred to it as moving "from glory to glory" (2 Cor. 3:18 NASB). And on that journey,

- in the Crowds, we experience that joy *listening to Christ* and *watching* him at work;
- in the Five Thousand, we experience it by *receiving from Christ;*
- in the Seventy, we find joy in *working for Christ;* and
- in the Twelve, we find the joy of *walking with Christ.*

Growing as a Christian might best be described as working on our joy and the joy of those around us. One day our final destination will be not only entering into heaven but entering into joy itself! And we'll hear, "Well done, good and faithful servant; you were faithful over a few things, I will make you ruler over many things. Enter into the joy of your lord" (Matt. 25:21 NKJV).

Remember . . . in the Twelve, the way of Jesus is the way of joy; to follow him is to follow joy.

28

One in Every Crowd

Greetings, Rabbi!

—JUDAS TO JESUS, MATTHEW 26:49 NKJV

Benedict Arnold was the most famous betrayer during the American Revolutionary War, but Judas was the one most remembered in the Bible, if not all of world history. The Roman Empire also produced a famous betrayer of its own named Marcus Brutus.

Brutus showed his true colors to the then emperor, Julius Caesar, early on when he took sides against the ruler with Caesar's chief rival and contender, Pompey. It happened during the Roman Civil War of 49–46 BC. After Pompey was defeated, Brutus relented and wrote a letter of apology to Caesar. Amazingly during such a period of upheaval and rebellion, Caesar forgave him and offered Brutus a position in his inner circle, making him governor of Gaul (now northern Italy).

In order to reassert his role in the region soon after the war,

Caesar proclaimed himself dictator for life over Rome. This action incensed many members of the Roman government and leadership. Eventually a conspiracy developed with the goal of assassinating the emperor, and Brutus was among the conspirators.

The assassination famously took place on March 15, 44 BC, a day known as the Ides of March. When Caesar came to meet with the Senate that day, they all suddenly turned on him. Recognizing Brutus was among them, Caesar resigned himself to his fate and raised his toga over his head. It is said so many attacked him that day that some of them inadvertently wounded one another with the flailing stabs of their knives.

Just as Caesar had a Brutus, Jesus had a Judas. By all accounts, Judas during his earliest months as a disciple had much the same experience and showed the same loyalties to Christ as did the rest of the Twelve. Just as the rest of the Twelve, Judas had been chosen by Christ, called by Christ, and he left his vocation in order to follow him. Judas was so trusted that he was given oversight of the disciples' treasury.

Somewhere along Judas's journey as a Christ follower, however, something went terribly awry to the point that Jesus predicted a betrayal. Jesus could see it coming, whether by divine revelation or the gradual emotional disconnection Judas exhibited. He fell so far away that he ultimately came to a day in which he was willing to literally sell Jesus out.

ANATOMY OF A BETRAYAL

Judas had enjoyed a front-row seat to Jesus' ministry. He got to see the miracles of Christ up close and personal. So what led to the unthreading of Judas's faith? How does such a betrayal occur? Could a Christ follower today fall prey to the same trap?

Luke told us that by the time of the Last Supper "Satan

entered into Judas . . . who was of the number of the Twelve" (Luke 22:3 ESV). The Bible gives us insights into the unraveling of Judas's faith walk; and how we might fall prey to some of the same temptation in ours if we are not careful:

He Listened to the Crowds More than to Christ

While Jesus was still speaking to the Three who accompanied him to Gethsemane, and while he cautioned them to pray that they "will not fall into temptation," Judas arrived on the scene with his posse (vv. 45–47). As Jesus was warning the Three about the risk of falling away, in walked one who had done just that. And he was not alone: "There came a crowd, and the man called Judas, one of the twelve, was leading them" (v. 47 ESV).

According to Luke, Judas had been seeking an opportunity "to betray [Jesus] to them in the absence of a crowd" (v. 6 ESV). John MacArthur characterized Judas in this way: "He was a coward. He knew the popularity of Jesus. He was afraid of the crowd. Like every hypocrite, he was obsessed with concerns about what people thought of him."[1]

His Faith Became an Act Instead of a Relationship

Jesus seemed astounded not merely by Judas's act of betrayal but also by how he went about it: "Judas, would you betray the Son of Man *with a kiss*?" (v. 48 NLT, emphasis mine). In other words, "Really, Judas? Are you going to betray me and all the while do so pretending to be my friend? You've lost your faith, but have you also lost your mind?" Matthew's account notes that Jesus also said to Judas, "Do what you came for, friend" (26:50). His passionate faith had turned to an empty and sickening religious show.

He Lost His Sense of What's Really Important

Three years earlier Judas had left everything to follow Jesus. Now, after conferring with the religious leaders so eager to entrap Christ, Judas sold that "everything" for thirty Roman coins. The chronology of the Gospels shows that Judas sold Jesus out right after his anointing at Bethany. Mary, the sister of Martha, broke open an expensive jar of perfume and poured it on Jesus' head and feet. While Jesus recognized Mary had done something "beautiful"[2] for him, Judas said such use of the precious perfume was a waste: "'Why wasn't this perfume sold and the money given to the poor? It was worth a year's wages.' He did not say this because he cared about the poor but because he was a thief; as keeper of the money bag, he used to help himself to what was put into it" (John 12:5–6).

While Jesus viewed what Mary did in a broad eternal manner, Judas saw it in a temporal one. While Jesus valued what Mary had done for his soul, Judas was concerned about what it had *not* done for their bank account. While Mary anointed him with extravagant love, Judas disappointed him with his excessive greed. He was using Christ for his own personal gain, but while he was gaining "the whole world" he was losing "his soul" (Matt. 16:26 ESV).

JUDAS AND ME

Before we assign shock and awe to the story of Judas and his treasonous behavior, we should ask: *Is there any Judas in me? Have I ever been willing to sell Jesus out? Or to sell him short in my life?*

History records that there was a day when Christ called, and Judas came out of the Crowds and into the Twelve. He followed Jesus, as did the other eleven. Something, however, never fully connected. While Judas came out of the Crowds, somehow the Crowds never quite came out of Judas. The first day he stopped pursuing Christ intentionally and passionately was the day he started falling behind. It would do us well to remember the chilling words Jesus used to describe Judas: "It would be better for him if he had not been born" (Mark 14:21).

Remember... in the Twelve, we are always doing one of two things: we are *following* or *falling back*.

PART 3

Knowing Christ,
the Friend

The Three

Knowing the Depths of Christ

"A place in the inner circle of Christ was something I wanted from the start. You may call me 'ambitious' or 'overly motivated' while others call me 'controlling,' 'greedy,' or 'entitled.' Nonetheless, I am not content to sit comfortably among the Twelve and desire nothing more. When he granted me the privilege of becoming one of the Three, I exulted over the honor and privilege this would represent. It was not long, however, before I would come to see that to whom much is given, much is required. I have come to find that the greater the privilege, the deeper the pain; the closer one comes to Christ and his joys, the closer one will come to his sufferings. Am I ready for the heights *and* the depths?"

29

Mama's Prayers

You don't know what you are asking.

—Matthew 20:22

A son can fill a mother's heart with absolute joy and, sometimes, great pain. One struggling mother, Monica, prayed often for her son that he would become a Christ follower. Monica's husband, however, was not a Christian and sometimes he mocked her prayers for her son as futile. Unfortunately the son inherited his father's cynicism and yet also had an astonishingly brilliant mind. His parents worked to send him off to school where he distinguished himself as an intellectual.

Even though her son's knowledge increased, his faith diminished further. In one exchange with his mother he told her he had determined Christ was not "divine" or "God incarnate." His words and his unbelief, though articulate in delivery, devastated his mother. Still, she continued to pray.

To make matters worse, the son decided to move in with his girlfriend, and the two of them had a son out of wedlock. When the mother sought the counsel of her minister about her prodigal son, he said, "The son of so many tears could never come to destruction." This statement encouraged Monica. So she prayed all the more, feeling she had received a *Life*Word from God.

THE HEIGHTS AND THE DEPTHS

When the mom of James and John asked that they "sit in places of honor next to [Jesus]" in his kingdom, she did so with specificity: "one on your right and the other on your left" (Matt. 20:21 NLT). She had a big request to make of Jesus, and the outcome is interesting.

While Jesus challenged the request made by Zebedee's wife, he did not flatly deny her. Not even close. On the contrary, it seems as if he were putting her and her sons through a bit of a disciple's checkpoint, helping them weigh the significance of their request. He asked them: "Can you drink the cup I am going to drink?" (v. 22).

The Three would indeed be exposed to unique privileges in the company of Christ, and true to his words, they would come face-to-face with the cup of suffering he was called upon to drink. The place of the Three is where we are drawn into Jesus' Passion. At this place in our journey our motivation is growing into the heights and depths of knowing Christ. *The Three represent those who are led to the places of suffering and glory with Christ.* Think of it this way:

In the Crowds, we *listen to Christ.*
In the Five Thousand, we *receive from Christ.*
In the Seventy, we *work for Christ.*

In the Twelve, we *walk with Christ*.

In the Three, we learn to *suffer and reign with Christ*.

This is shown by the two places where Jesus took the Three exclusively. The rest of the Twelve were not included.

Jesus led the Three *to the heights*, to the Mount of Transfiguration. One of the most heavenly and mysterious experiences of Christ recorded in the Gospels is his transfiguration. In many ways it portrays a moment of touching heaven while on earth. This moment seems to be a sneak preview of the consummation of Christ as well as a final affirmation from heaven just before the events of Christ's Passion.

Jesus led the Three *to the depths*, to the Garden of Gethsemane. One of the most earthly, human, and challenging experiences of Christ in the record of the Gospels was his agonizing prayer in the Garden of Gethsemane on the eve of his arrest and trial. While Calvary represents the inestimable physical suffering of Christ, arguably Gethsemane was chief among his emotional struggles and sufferings. It appears his wrestling was more with his humanity at this event ("If it is possible, may this cup be taken from me" [Matt. 26:39]); he struggled under such intense stress that "his sweat became like great drops of blood falling down to the ground" (Luke 22:44 ESV) in the process. It seems the cup Jesus had warned James, John, and their mother about, he was starting to taste.

And consider just who comprised the Three: Simon Peter and a certain mother's two sons. Remember her? The opening chapter of this book was all about her bold prayer of asking Jesus to let her sons be as close to him as possible. Well, God answered her prayer. Yes, he did. Have you noticed yet? Her sons James and John were two of the Three who formed the inner circle of Christ.

When the mother of James and John first made her bold request of Jesus, neither she nor her sons really knew what they were asking. It is quite clear they wanted power, prestige, influence, and a place in the inner cabinet of Jesus the moment he wrested power from the Romans and established himself as king. Undoubtedly self-aggrandizement was a part of this request or prayer, but the way Jesus engaged it revealed something more.

Henri Nouwen recognized the mother's answered prayer:

> James and John . . . hardly understood who Jesus was. They didn't think about him as a leader who would be betrayed, tortured, and killed on a cross. Nor did they dream about their own lives as marked by tiresome travels and harsh persecutions, and consumed by contemplation or martyrdom. Their first easy yes had to be followed by many hard yeses until their cups were completely empty. . . .
>
> Still, notwithstanding all their misperceptions, they had been deeply touched by this man Jesus. In his presence they had experienced something radically new, something that went beyond anything they had ever imagined. It had to do with inner freedom, love, care, hope, and most of all, with God. Yes, they wanted power and influence, but beyond that they wanted to stay close to Jesus at all costs.[1]

JESUS HAD A PLAN—DISCIPLESHIP

James and John were called closely into the life of Christ, into the Three. Leonard Sweet cites the fact that Jesus had a clear plan and strategy for changing lives through discipleship:

> Jesus did have a plan for discipling his followers, in other words, a two-part strategic initiative. The first step of Plan A was that his disciples would "be with him." The first step of Plan B was that he would "send them out."
>
> . . . The plan was not to spend the major focus on gathering crowds together to hear him speak. Jesus' plan, instead,

was for a few people to be deeply involved and participate in his actual life, sharing in the way that he carried out his life and sharing their lives with him as well. And then, when they had absorbed his very life within them, he would send . . . them out into the culture to be his body in the world.[2]

Monica, the mom mentioned earlier in this chapter, got much older, and yet she continued to pray for her wayward son. Eventually he became frustrated with the life he had made and with himself. Questioning God more vigorously, he went back to church and started to read the Bible. One day he came to his mother to inform her that he had received Christ as his Savior. On Easter that year, she watched her son and grandson get baptized. That autumn, she breathed her last and slipped into the arms of the one to whom she had prayed for her son so much.

And her son's name?

Augustine.

Better known to most people as Saint Augustine. His writings would become a fire that would light the heart of Martin Luther and set the world aflame for the gospel. Perhaps Augustine's most famous quotation is an epitaph to his life: "Our hearts are restless until they find their rest in thee, O Lord."[3]

Augustine found himself in the intimate circles of Christ. Apparently so did James and John. Where would the world be without praying moms?

Remember . . . in the Three, we follow Christ to the places of suffering and glory, to the depths and the heights.

30

Mountain View Lodge

*He did not let anyone follow except
Peter, James and John.*

—MARK 5:37

When it comes to our walk with Christ, the Three represent the inner circle of Christ. Theologians have long referred to this group as the Triumvirate, the Three disciples closest to Christ. And in our journey closer, *the Three represent those who have followed Jesus to the places of suffering (or struggle) and glory (or privilege).*

One of these privileged places was what has come to be known as the Mount of Transfiguration. The Three were the only ones privileged to follow Christ to this place. After asking his disciples, "Who do you say I am?" (Luke 9:20) and calling them to the next level in their faith, Jesus took Peter, James, and John on a little expedition: "[Jesus] took Peter, John and James with him and went up onto a mountain to pray. As he was praying, the appearance of his face changed, and his clothes became as bright as a flash of lightning. Two men, Moses and Elijah, appeared in glorious splendor, talking with Jesus. They spoke about his departure, which he was about to bring to fulfillment at Jerusalem" (vv. 28–31).

The transfiguration event itself is like nothing else in all of Scripture. Perhaps the thing that comes closest to it was when Moses ventured up the mountain of God and returned so charged with God's presence that his face glowed or shone (Ex. 34:35). But the word used here represents something more than a reflection; it is a transformation or transfiguration. Jesus, if but for a moment, changed or metamorphosed before their eyes. Although certainly far more glorious, it was perhaps somewhat like the scene of someone on *Star Trek* being beamed from one location to another. The original word used by Luke (Gk: *exastrapto*) means Jesus' clothing became dazzling white like lightning itself.

The story continued: "Peter and his companions were very sleepy, but when they became fully awake, they saw his glory and the two men standing with him. As the men were leaving Jesus, Peter said to him, 'Master, it is good for us to be here. Let us put up three shelters—one for you, one for Moses and one for Elijah.' (He did not know what he was saying.)" (Luke 9:32–33).

Peter had a "suggestion." Once again, he had an idea and blurted it out. While Peter wanted to memorialize this moment, Jesus wanted to maximize it. Peter wanted this glorious moment to be frozen in time; Jesus wanted it to fill and prepare him and the other two for the challenges of the dark valley that lay ahead.

The focal point of the follower at the place of the Three is *the ways of God*. Only it seems it wasn't the ways of God that Peter seemed most concerned about at that point. Peter could have stayed right up there on that mountain. For Peter, it was a Christian retreat center in the making; for Jesus, it was a momentary respite and recharge to prepare him for the challenges, struggles, sufferings, and conquests that lay ahead of him in the valley with yet another mountain to climb. This one was called Calvary.

PETER'S PASSION

In studying Peter and his journey of following Christ, we could certainly describe it as a passionate journey. What Peter lacked in areas of tactfulness and patience, he at times made up for in fervor, response, and attention to the moment. Alexander Whyte summed it up well:

> With all his faults, and he was full of them, a cold heart was not one of them. All Peter's faults, indeed, lay in the heat of his heart. He was too hot-hearted, too impulsive, too enthusiastic. His hot heart was always in his mouth, and he spoke it all out many a time when he should have held his peace. So many faults had Peter, . . . that you might very easily take a too hasty and a too superficial estimate of Peter's real depth and strength and value. And if Peter was too long like the sand rather than like the rock his Master had so nobly named him, the sand will one day settle into rock, and into rock of a quality and a quantity to build a temple with.[1]

The Transfiguration is a miracle, yes, but uniquely among the works of Christ this is not one Jesus performed on someone else. It was a miracle he experienced in his body. The Transfiguration is considered one of the milestones in the life and ministry of Christ in the Gospels, which include his

- baptism,
- transfiguration,
- crucifixion,

- resurrection, and
- ascension.

You might say these are the five big-ticket events that mark major moments and movements in the life and body of Christ. They are of such significance that, in a sense, they are replicated in our spiritual formation as Christ followers.

We experience a baptism as identification with the birth of Christ into the world and his death. He entered our world at the incarnation; we enter his kingdom at our conversion to Christ, salvation. Jesus taught that "unless one is born again he cannot see the kingdom of God" (John 3:3 NASB). In this experience we are born into Christ.

We experience a transfiguration as identification with the growth and maturing of Christ. As he was transfigured before the eyes of his disciples, so "we all, with unveiled face, beholding the glory of the Lord, are being transformed [Greek, *metamorphoo*] into the same image from one degree of glory to another" (2 Cor. 3:18 ESV).[2] We are changed by Christ.

We experience a crucifixion as identification with the suffering of Christ. As Christ died on the cross to bring us salvation, so we die with him on our little crosses to bring him a life of surrender and obedience. Paul said, "I have been crucified with Christ and I no longer live, but Christ lives in me" (Gal. 2:20). Christ died to himself for our sake; now we are called to die to ourselves for his sake.

We experience a resurrection as identification with the overcoming power of Christ. As the faith of Christ helped him overcome death, hell, and the grave, so our faith in Christ keeps us overcoming challenges, struggles, and enemies in this life: "Since you have been raised to new life with Christ, set your sights on the realities of heaven, where Christ sits in the place of honor at God's right hand" (Col. 3:1 NLT). We are risen with Christ.

We will experience ascension as identification with the ultimate victory of Christ. While the ascension of Christ may not necessarily bring us to every mountaintop we desire in life, it provides us access to all those God has ordained and to the ultimate one, the mountain of the Lord. As Christ followers, one day we will ascend to Christ.

These five experiences of Christ reveal important ways God grows and conforms us more and more to the image of Christ. In a sense each of these events represents another mountain God calls us to climb in his name—baptism, transfiguration, crucifixion, resurrection, and ascension. However, we must not allow ourselves to get stuck at any one of these places; rather, we must press on toward maturity and wholeness in Christ.

Remember ... in the Three, we not only remember the events in Jesus' life; we enter into those events in ours.

31

Cloudy Christianity

Jesus never promised his followers an easy life.[1]

—DAVID WATSON

The Christian life includes clouds. Have you noticed?

When Peter ascended the Mount of Transfiguration with Jesus, James, and John, something really different occurred, something cloudy:

> Peter said to Jesus, "Rabbi, it is good for us to be here. Let us put up three shelters—one for you, one for Moses and one for Elijah." (He did not know what to say, they were so frightened.)
>
> *Then a cloud appeared and covered them, and a voice came from the cloud*: "This is my Son, whom I love. Listen to him!"
>
> Suddenly, when they looked around, they no longer saw anyone with them except Jesus. (Mark 9:5–8, emphasis mine)

In this case, as in the episode of Peter walking on the water and then sinking (Matt. 14:22–33), it seems Peter's focus moved to the wrong place. Instead of giving Jesus his worship and attention, he seemed more enamored with Moses and Elijah and his own idea of what should come next ("Let us put up three shelters" [Mark 9:5]). Instead of granting his request, however, God covered all of them, first with a cloud and then with his voice. The result? "Suddenly, when they looked around, they no longer saw anyone . . . except Jesus" (v. 8). And isn't that as it should be? Aren't the best times in the Christian life those when our lives and activities are so clouded that all we can see is Christ?

Although God appeared to Moses as a "fire" in the burning bush (Ex. 3), Exodus 13:22 tells us that in the wilderness God came to the nation of Israel as a "pillar of cloud by day" and as a "pillar of fire by night." Israel's journey reveals important insights for us today:

God's presence came in the form of a cloud. As soon as Moses finished constructing the portable house of worship in the wilderness for the Hebrew nation (the tabernacle), the first thing God did was to send a "cloud" to cover it (Num. 9:15). One day God even spoke to Moses and said, "I am going to come to you in a dense cloud, so that the people will hear me speaking with you and will always put their trust in you" (Ex. 19:9).

At night, the cloud took on the appearance of fire. The cloud somehow morphed or changed as night set in: "At evening it was over the tabernacle like the appearance of fire until morning" (Num. 9:15 ESV).

The people of God were to move only when the cloud moved. As long as the cloud remained over the tabernacle, the people were supposed to stay put. When the cloud moved, they moved. They moved only with the cloud, that is, the presence of God.

God came as a cloud every time Moses went up on Mount Sinai. When Moses walked up the mountain to meet with God, in a sense he was walking into a cloud. Moses' most intimate times in the presence of God were cloudy experiences.

My Journey Toward the Three

Every closeness life affords us includes corresponding privileges and prices. James, John, and Peter would find that out.

For many years as a follower of Christ, I have prayed to know Christ more, to follow him more fully, and to experience him and his presence more deeply. But as a younger follower I did not understand God would use struggles, challenges, and even unexpected clouds to help answer that prayer.

One cloud God used to open me up to more of him was an unexpected struggle with my voice when I was a young husband and parent. For six months, talking became extremely difficult. Simple one-on-one discussions were a challenge. Also, trying to figure it all out was putting a strain on my spirit, my marriage, and my family. The scariest part was I felt as if I had lost something I assumed I would always have—a strong, clear, and resonant voice.

The most challenging part of this season was my questions: "God, why is this going on? Why don't you just heal me? You called me to preach, and now I'm having a hard time just talking. What is the deal with that?" Little did I know God was allowing something for a time to be removed because of something he wanted to add.

THE GUIDE OF THE CLOUD

Clouds can do really good things:

Clouds Provide Shade

Clouds offer shade from the blistering and harsh rays of the sun: "God spread a cloud to keep them cool through the day and a fire to light their way through the night" (Ps. 105:41 MSG). In a desert, a cloud is no disappointment; rather, it is a grace gift. God is our shade.

Clouds Sometimes Bring Rain

Clouds are often God's fountain of thirst-quenching water: "[God] causes his sun to rise on the evil and the good, and sends rain on the righteous and the unrighteous" (Matt. 5:45). Rain has often been turned into a metaphor for something bad in our culture, but in biblical times, it was a sign of blessing.

Clouds Can Be a Guide

When clouds and darkness come into our lives, it is easy to fear because of the unknown and of what we cannot see. However, David said to God:

> *Even the darkness will not be dark to you;*
> *the night will shine like the day,*
> *for darkness is as light to you. (Ps. 139:12)*

When I lost my voice for a year, it was difficult for me to believe anything good would ever come of it. After twelve years of preaching, teaching, and singing, I was struggling to do the thing I enjoyed most—communicate. The experience was often deeply frustrating and embarrassing. Since I was having trouble talking, I wrote. I wrote so much that within a few months I had penned three book manuscripts, one of them on the role of great questions in effective parenting.

The more I wrote, the more I felt the desire to see these materials published and read. But that seemed far out of reach. Soon, however, I felt compelled to ask, seek, and knock on a door or two. After several weeks with no response, I was ready to give up. Just about that time, I got a call from an editor at Focus on the Family: "We don't want to do a book with you, Bob. Actually we want to do *two*. How would you feel about that?"

Something in me exploded in that moment. I think you call it joy. God had just opened an exciting door at one of the lowest seasons in my life. Since then he has opened more doors for my writing voice than I could have imagined. The first two books I had published are now called "Conversation Starters," and ironically they are loaded with questions to help people all over the world do something I was struggling with at the time—*talk* with each other.

CONSIDERING THE CLOUDS

I have found God still often comes in the clouds. Mark's gospel tells us his second coming will be in the same way: "At that time people will see the Son of Man coming in clouds with great power and glory" (13:26).

Although my voice has not completely recovered, it is much improved. To this day there remains a little residue of brokenness in the tone, not enough to keep me from teaching and preaching—I do lots of both—but enough to remind me of how much I gained the year something in my life was taken away and to keep me telling this story. Sometimes God has to send a cloud over one area of our lives to open our eyes to the light he is shining on other things he wants us to do, things we have not yet seen or imagined.

Remember . . . in the Three, as the clouds around us get darker, we begin to hear God's voice clearer.

32

Disney's Dynamic Duo

A disciple is only a disciple if he shares
Christ's life, including his pain, his suffering,
his rejection, even his crucifixion.[1]

—DAVID WATSON

No filmmaker has been more prolific than Walt Disney. To date, the organization he founded on the heels of a cute little rodent, namely Mickey Mouse, has produced more than six hundred feature films.

No one could produce such a catalog of creative materials and enterprises as did Disney without a keen understanding of what goes into making a great story. For Disney there were two essentials to every film. Out of these he developed a model that served him well. Whenever he veered from it, his films suffered at the box office; when he kept to it, they generally did much better. You could call the essentials Disney's Dynamic Duo.

The two most important ingredients for any film were that somehow the main character or characters had to experience two things: intense suffering of some sort and also ecstatic joy. Disney found these two humanizing components caused audiences to identify with and connect to the stories and characters he made famous. Interestingly enough, these were the two dynamics Jesus seemed to prioritize with the Three. You could say that *the Three represent those who follow Jesus to the places of suffering and joy,* to the Garden of Gethsemane and to the Mount of Transfiguration.

An important aspect of growing in Christ is coming to know him in his life and his life experiences. As we do, we identify with Jesus. Theologians call this concept *identification with Christ.* The apostle Paul called it *knowing Christ*: "I want to know Christ—yes, to know the power of his resurrection and participation in his sufferings, becoming like him in his death, and so, somehow, attaining to the resurrection from the dead" (Phil. 3:10–11).

In other words, as we come to "know Christ" we come to experience and know more of the things he went through, such as "the power of his resurrection," "his sufferings," and so on. Jesus took the Three—Peter, James, and John—to deep and powerful places of experience and emotion that were unique from the experiences shared by the other disciples. In some ways, they were highly privileged to go to these places with him; in others, they were deeply challenged. Jesus took the Three to the heights and to the depths.

When Jesus took the Three to the Mount of Transfiguration, he was inviting them to catch a sneak peek of his glory. There was no moment or experience more heavenly and otherworldly than this mountaintop one. By taking them to this place, Jesus was showing the Three his panoramic connection to the law

(Moses) and the prophets (Elijah) and the grand fulfillment of God's kingdom purpose.

When Jesus took the Three to the Garden of Gethsemane, he was inviting them to stand with him in his suffering. On the night he would be arrested, Jesus went away to pray. By that time the atmosphere in and around Jerusalem was thick with tension. Some wanted to worship Jesus; others wanted to stone him. The weight of the coming cross weighing heavily on his soul, he wanted or needed to pray. Frequently Jesus went to "lonely places" all by himself to spend time with the heavenly Father and pray (Luke 5:16). Not that time, however. He asked the Three to come along with him. He was calling Peter, James, and John to share in his prayer and his suffering.

CONFIDANTS

True friends rejoice with us when we rejoice and weep with us when we weep. They stand with us in our joys and struggles. Growing in Christ brings a deepening to our knowledge of Jesus but also to our emotional posture toward him. For instance:

- in the Crowds, we hear about Jesus amid *culture*;
- in the Five Thousand, we *consume* the gifts and blessings of Christ;
- in the Seventy, we become *colaborers* with Christ in his work;
- in the Twelve, we join him as *comrades* or companions on his journey; but
- in the Three, we become the *confidants* of Christ in his sufferings and victories. We share in his passions, his ups and downs, his heights and depths.

Emotions: The Colors of the Soul

Emotions are vital parts of our faith and faith experiences. Emotions are the colors of the soul. Although they add vibrancy to our lives and faith experiences, we must not be consumed or controlled by our emotions.

Jesus showed concern for two things in the lives, hearts, and minds of those who would follow him closely. If I put them in questions he would ask us, I believe they would be these:

1. "Are you ready for your heart to be filled with joys it has never known?"
2. "Are you prepared for your heart to be torn into pieces by struggles and challenges?"

When you really love someone, you are willing to follow him to the heights and the depths. The ups and downs. For better, for worse. You are intimately interested in his greatest joys and deepest sorrows. Paul the apostle also affirmed this when he admonished Christ followers to "rejoice with those who rejoice, and weep with those who weep" (Rom. 12:15 NASB). To "rejoice with those who rejoice" is to share in their joy; to "weep with those who weep" is to share in their suffering.

Walt Disney knew that to make great stories, he would have to create great characters and help people fall in love with them. The readers and viewers would have to come closer to the main characters' joys and sorrows. When this occurred, a connection was made, and a great story was told.

Growing as a Christ follower, coming closer to Jesus, requires knowing more of his story, the joys and the sorrows, the heights and the depths, and sharing in them. As we enter into the good news of Jesus, we are transformed and transfixed by the Son of

God who takes away our sins and keeps calling us to come closer and to go deeper.

Remember … in the Three, we are drawn deeper into the Passion of Christ, into his joys and sorrows.

33

Weeping with Christ

Before we drink the cup, we must hold it![1]

—HENRI NOUWEN

The mother of James and John had a question for Jesus, but he also had one for them: "Can you drink from the cup that I'm going to drink from?" (Matt. 20:22 ISV). As Christ followers we are called to live the events of our lives in the light of Jesus' life.

The apostle Paul found strength and power to persevere by identifying consistently with Jesus and the events in his life. Paul tracked the events of his life and the lives of his fellow Christ followers in light of the pivotal events in Christ's. Just listen to what he said:

"I want to know Christ and the power of his *resurrection* and the fellowship of sharing in his *sufferings*, becoming like him in his *death*, and so, somehow, to attain to the *resurrection* from the dead" (Phil. 3:10–11, emphasis mine).

Our faith in Christ is not a magic wand we use to get what we want. Rather, it is a divine enablement God places within us to help us become what he wants. Faith is the "God magnet" that keeps drawing us through our life journeys and closer to Jesus. Faith is a powerful and forceful tool, which includes many dimensions. For example,

in the Crowds, we experience a hearing faith;
in the Five Thousand, we experience a tasting faith;
in the Seventy, we experience a serving faith;
in the Twelve, we experience a following faith; but
in the Three, we experience a deepening faith.

A Personal Gethsemane?

Life includes Gethsemane experiences. Have you noticed? Our Gethsemanes are those places where our will wrestles to find its way to God's will. As Adam represented mankind by wrestling his way *out* of God's will through disobedience, so Jesus represented us by wrestling his way *into* God's will by obedience (1 Cor. 15:45–49).

Our Gethsemane is the place where we count the cost, where we consider what it will demand of us to go the way God is calling—all the way. We ponder and we pray. We sweat and we struggle. We weep and we wonder. We play out the scenes of what will be required of us as we follow him.

The Stress

As Jesus looked in the Garden at what he faced in his life, so great was his stress that he said, "My soul is overwhelmed with sorrow to the point of death" (Matt. 26:38).

Not only did Jesus take my place and yours on the cross;

he also took our place at Gethsemane. If Calvary was the place he bore our physical pain and suffering, it seems Gethsemane is where he bore the psychological trauma of it. Make no mistake; *I* was supposed to be there, and so were *you*. The emotional struggle was not over his sins, but yours and mine that he took upon himself. He wasn't fighting for himself that night; he was fighting for you and me.

In the Garden that dark night, Jesus asked Peter, James, and John to stay and watch with him in prayer, but they did not (Matt 26:38, 40). He wanted them to share in his sufferings (Phil. 3:10) and to behold the depths of his struggle so they might perceive the depths of his love. But they missed the moment.

Notice what Jesus said when they fell asleep. Mark wrote, "[Jesus] came and found them sleeping, and he said to Peter, '*Simon*, are you asleep? Could you not watch one hour?'" (14:37–38 ESV, emphasis mine). It was not a "Rock" moment in Peter's journey, not even close. On that occasion Jesus called him "Simon" instead. It must have felt somewhat like a parent formally calling us by our full given names rather than by our affectionate nicknames.

THE STRUGGLE

Certainly Gethsemane was a place of struggle for Jesus. But what was he struggling with? Was it the weight of the world and its sin? Most definitely. But there was something else.

A careful and honest reading of the text shows that his struggle was also with the will of God. He prayed, "My Father, if it is possible, may this cup be taken from me" (Matt. 26:39).

Couldn't there be another way? How many times have you asked God that question? I know I have, countless times. Take comfort in the fact that on this occasion, Jesus did also.

Henri Nouwen wrote about the "cup" Jesus asked James, John, and their mother if they could "drink":

Holding the cup of life is a hard discipline. We are thirsty people who like to start drinking at once. But we need to restrain our impulse to drink, put both of our hands around the cup, and ask ourselves, "What am I given to drink? What is in my cup? . . ."

. . . No two lives are the same. We often compare our lives with those of others, trying to decide whether we are better or worse off, but such comparisons do not help us much. We have to live our life, not someone else's. We have to hold *our own* cup.[2]

For you and for me, Gethsemane is a place of coming to terms with the will of God. It is a place where we face God's will head-on. At Gethsemane, we look honestly and clearly at what God has called us to do. We consider the call, and we count the cost.

We go into our Gethsemanes with a plea, hoping for a Plan B. But we go in looking through the wrong lens. We are missing the true colors. We eventually find that Gethsemane is not about changing the will of God to fit our lifestyle, whims, and wishes; rather, it is about changing our minds, our expectations, our lifestyles, and our plans to fit his will. It is not a place of petition; rather, it is one of surrender.

Gethsemane is not the cross. It is not the place where we die. Rather, it is the place where we are told we are *going* to die—die to self that we might live for God; die to our ways that we might live in his.

THE STEEL

Gethsemane for Jesus was the place where he collected himself and set his face firmly in the direction of God's will. Like steel refined, Gethsemane provided Jesus (as it provides you and me) with a place to pour out his questions and concerns, and to cast all his cares and anxieties upon a loving heavenly Father. Nouwen noted that the answers Jesus needed to find at Gethsemane "couldn't be felt in the body, nor thought through in the mind. But it was there," he wrote. "It was that spiritual sinew, that intimate communion with his Father that made him hold on to the cup and pray."[3]

JESUS ID

Something happened in Jesus' soul at Gethsemane, something he wants us to experience as his followers. At Gethsemane he modeled for us what he wants us to learn to do regularly: "Cast all your anxiety on him because he cares for you" (1 Peter 5:7).

Resisting temptation involves using our faith to struggle our way through the challenges. We come upon barriers at every level of our growth in Christ we must steadfastly resist and overcome. The barrier we face . . .

in the Crowds is our *unbelief*;
in the Five Thousand is our *selfishness*;
in the Seventy is *the works trap*;
in the Twelve is our *self-will*; but
in the Three is our *prayerlessness*.

Gethsemane is a place where we struggle with ourselves, our selfishness, our wants, our hopes, our dreams and disappointments. It is where we lose ourselves to find the new person God is making; not just new resolve, but a new life, a new identity in Christ. Oswald Chambers stated, "Our Lord is trying to introduce us to identification with Himself through a particular 'Gethsemane' experience of our own."[4] And remember, every Gethsemane leads to a resurrection but not before it first leads to a cross.

Remember ... in the Three, we come to see our struggles
not as difficult events that isolate us from God but
as challenges that help us draw closer to him.

34

Cowboy Disciple

You do not know what kind of spirit you are of.

—LUKE 9:55 NASB

One of my favorite movies of all time is *Top Gun*. The main character of the film has the nickname Maverick and for good reason. He is a hot dog, a showboat, and a rugged individualist if there ever was one; he is just the kind of guy who gives commanding officers ulcers.

In the film, Maverick's bullheadedness causes problems for several people around him. The tension in the story is ultimately not something on the outside but the demons of his past on the inside.

Jesus surrounded himself with three Mavericks. We all know Peter had that reputation. But at the start, James and John were no different. While we traditionally tend to picture John the Beloved as a mild-mannered man, he more likely had explosive tendencies. As a matter of fact, John was so determined that early on Jesus referred to him as one of the "Sons of Thunder." In other words, John and his brother James were so bullheaded and explosive that it was as if Thunder itself fathered or birthed them onto the planet.

THUNDER BOYS

No episode reveals James and John's tendency toward self-will and explosive reaction any more than what they did soon after coming down from the Mount of Transfiguration. Since they were heading back to Jerusalem with Jesus, they knew cutting through Samaria would save them lots of time. When they started the journey, Jesus sent messengers ahead to the next Samaritan village to prepare a place for them to lodge. The townspeople, however, refused to receive them. That response, no doubt, was connected to the long-standing prejudices between the Samaritans and the Jews.

James and John's reaction was immediate and ultimate: "Lord, should we call down fire from heaven to burn them up?" (Luke 9:54 NLT).

How many of us are pretty sure we would not have wanted to face that kind of temperament from a boss, a dad, or even a principal at our school for that matter? Wow! Where did that come from? "Burn them up?" Wherever it came from, one thing is for sure, Jesus immediately confronted it. His confrontation was reminiscent of the time Peter tried to rebuke Jesus, and Jesus responded with a "Get behind me, Satan" retort. His response to James and John was similar: "He turned and rebuked them, and said, 'You do not know what kind of spirit you are of'" (v. 55 NASB).

A few questions arise as I consider this event:

1. What were James and John thinking? Where did they get such an idea?
2. What kind of king did they think they were serving?
3. What kind of kingdom were they building?
4. What does this incident reveal about the will of God and the ways of God?

PYROMANIA?

"Call down fire from heaven"? Where did these guys get such an idea? I mean, we see Jesus before this event bringing sight to blind eyes, food to the hungry, and mobility to disabled limbs, along with so many other miracles, but never do we see him calling down fire upon the heads of people. What an outrageous request, one that doesn't sound too different from throwing a hand grenade or pointing a flamethrower in someone's direction.

Yet to find the source of this idea, one only needs to consider the men whom James and John saw standing with Jesus on the Mount of Transfiguration and talking with him. Next to Jesus were the prophet Elijah and the patriarch Moses, no less. So, in addition to seeing Moses, the Sons of Thunder got ringside seats to see Elijah, whom many consider the greatest of the Old Testament prophets. And do you remember one of the things Elijah was noted for? It was calling down fire out of heaven at Mount Carmel at the showdown with the false prophets—the Smackdown of the Millennium where Elijah proved the God who came in fire was the true God.

After only a few hours with the great prophet on a mountain, the Sons of Thunder were suddenly ready to get their Elijah on. It sounds as if in the face of the Samaritan resistance, James and John felt holstered up with supernatural six-shooters and were ready to unload on anyone who dared stand in their way. These guys sound more like a couple of bouncers for a mobster than clergymen in the making, don't they? More prepared for the streets of Chicago in the 1920s than the humble fields of ancient Palestine.

James and John at that point, much as Peter did, were developing the wrong ideas about this King (Jesus) and about the kind of kingdom he was determined to build. They were more impressed with the power of God than they were with the God of power. There is a big difference. Jesus' followers somewhat misperceived the authority he possessed and used to teach the masses and to heal the sick. They assumed the deeds of goodness and grace were only precursors of the power and force that would soon be exhibited to topple the rulers of the day and place Jesus on the throne. In their minds, they could see a King David returning to his rightful throne in the immediate future.

THE WILL AND THE WAY

This altercation reveals something vital about God and his kingdom plan. We have a tendency to focus our spiritual pursuits on the will of God, but God wants us not only to know and do his *will* but also to do his will his *way*. Trying to do God's will our way makes it no longer God's will. Isaiah recorded this statement from God about this subject:

> "My thoughts are not your thoughts,
>   neither are your ways my ways,"
>   declares the LORD.
> "As the heavens are higher than the earth,
>   so are my ways higher than your ways
>   and my thoughts than your thoughts."
>   (ISA. 55:8–9)

REACT OR RESPOND

It just may be that all of us have a bit of the maverick within us, in the sense that we get stuck in our own ways and selfishness. The last I checked, *selfishness* is synonymous with *sinfulness*. Our fallen nature and selfish bent pull us toward sin. Christ and the work of his Spirit in our lives through spiritual formation are conforming us into the image of Christ, into a life that embraces and reflects both the will and the ways of God.

C. S. Lewis summed up the struggle of that formation this way: "Though our feelings come and go, His love for us does not. It is not wearied by our sins, or our indifference; and, therefore, it is quite relentless in its determination that we shall be cured of those sins, at whatever cost to us, at whatever cost to Him."[1]

Angered at the rejection of the Samaritans, James and John wanted to take power into their own hands. They wanted to use Jesus' power to zap those guys. Apparently they forgot the part about bless your enemies and turn the other cheek. They were not responding to Christ but instead reacting to a perceived problem. When we respond to Christ and his leading, we walk in the Spirit. When we react to life and its circumstances, we grieve God, and we miss his will and his way.

Remember ... in the Three, we become more impressed with the God of power than the power of God.

35

Speechless

They . . . said not one thing to anyone.

—Luke 9:36 MSG

When I went through the struggle with my voice several years ago, just talking one-on-one with someone was quite a challenge. Since I was a pastor of a growing congregation, the problem was exacerbated and, quite frankly, often embarrassing. I attended a large leadership conference and was getting ready to leave the hotel room with Pam and go to a meal in a large, and most likely noisy, banquet hall.

Since the speaking challenge I faced was making it hard to project my voice, a noisy room made it virtually impossible for me to be heard. But I knew our lives and our ministry needed to move ahead. Frustrated and discouraged, I remember how my wife, Pamela, tried to encourage me. By then, the voice challenge had been going on for months. By God's grace I was continuing to preach, and the church was continuing to grow, but something inside me was desperate for a word from God, a healing, or a sign of God's goodness.

I was in a place that might best be described as speechless.

What did Moses, Elijah, and Jesus say to each other on the Mount of Transfiguration? Don't you wonder?

Well, the Bible tells us of at least one subject on the conversation lineup that day: "They were speaking about his *exodus* from this world, which was about to be fulfilled in Jerusalem" (Luke 9:31 NLT, emphasis mine).

I WONDER

Since we are not privy to the details of this discussion, let me just say that one day in heaven I would like to ask permission to download this conversation and give it a good listen. Mostly I want to hear it because of what I think might have occurred. Here are my thoughts about it:

I wonder if Moses and Elijah were sent by the Father to encourage Jesus just before he began to face the most difficult days of his journey on earth.

I wonder in part because Moses certainly knew all about difficult journeys.

I wonder if these men who had faced such challenges atop mountains, Moses on Sinai and Elijah on Carmel, were here to help Jesus prepare for another one called Calvary.

I wonder if God the Father wanted the Son to see something only his sacrifice on the cross could ever make possible, namely Moses finally getting to set his bare feet on the promised land. His sins at the waters of Meribah had made that impossible before.

I wonder if Moses and Elijah brought any words of advice to Jesus on dealing with issues of crowd control? After all, Moses had led an entire nation across the wilderness, and Elijah had stared down another crowd with his confrontations and calls to commitment.

I wonder if these men talked at all to Jesus about dealing with godless rulers since in a short time Jesus would face the likes of Pontius Pilate. Did Moses talk about his confrontations with Pharaoh or Elijah his run-ins with the likes of Ahab and Jezebel?

Although my attempt to consider the conversation most certainly falls short of what really happened, we do know they talked about Jesus' final leg of the race, about his exodus from the earth and his mission to heaven and his position there. So, while their specific words are hidden from us, this visit on a mountain with Moses and Elijah likely involved encouragement, conversation, preparation, impartation, and a demonstration of the Father's devotion to his Son during this final climactic Passion of Christ.

But second, what did *Peter* say on that mountain?

This we know for certain. Here are his words: "When Moses and Elijah had left, Peter said to Jesus, 'Master, this is a great moment! Let's build three memorials: one for you, one for Moses, and one for Elijah.' He blurted this out without thinking" (v. 33 MSG).

IT'S SURPRISING

What surprises me at this moment is not what Peter said but what he *did not* say, such as "What is going on here?"

Remember what just occurred. After all, do you really think if you were on a mountain with Jesus and you saw his body become luminescent with glorious light and then you saw Moses and Elijah appear via some *Back to the Future* miracle, you are going to get up and give Jesus your plans on how you might *improve* on that moment? What would you call that?

How about *preposterous*? Peter missed the moment. And that was when God the Father showed up, and not a minute too soon: "As [Peter] was saying these things, a cloud came and over-shadowed them, and they were afraid as they entered the cloud. And a voice came out of the cloud, saying, *'This is my Son, my Chosen One; listen to him!'* And when the voice had spoken, Jesus was found alone" (vv. 34–36 ESV, emphasis mine).

The climax of this scene was not anything Moses or Elijah said to Jesus but the voice of his Father. And he had words with Peter, James, and John: "This is my Son, my Chosen One; listen to him!"

The irony was that Peter was on a mountain surrounded by one who parted the waters of the Red Sea, one who called fire down from heaven, and the one whose name is above all names, and all Peter could do was offer a suggestion on improving the moment. Need I say more?

That night in the hotel room before going to the dinner, Pamela continued to work hard at encouraging me. All dressed up, I sat in a chair in the corner of the room, not at all ready to go.

Then she said something I will never forget: "Robert, God knows how much you are struggling with this problem. And I believe there is something he wants to say to you to make sure you hear and hear deeply."

"And what's that?" I struggled to ask.

"That before you are a pastor," Pam said, "and before you are a husband, and before you are a dad, more than anything else *you are a son he dearly loves,* and he wants you to know how deeply and how very strongly he loves you and is with you through all of this."

Somewhere amid those soul-piercing words the tears started to flow. That was when the brokenness became ever so clear. And that, I believe, was when the healing began. That was when

I experienced that God often speaks the loudest in the moments in which we are at a loss for words.

In the final analysis, it isn't any particular words on the Mount of Transfiguration we most remember, but two things may be the biggest miracles of all that day:

Miracle #1: Jesus' body was vividly transformed but for a moment.

Miracle #2: "[Peter was] speechless" (v. 36 MSG). A miracle for certain!

Remember... in the Three, we discover what God desires from his followers is not another speech but an attitude of worship that leaves us speechless.

The One

Experiencing the Death and Life of Christ

"How did I find myself here standing alone with Jesus? Everywhere else I have been with him on this journey of faith has included other companions, sometimes even multitudes. I never asked to be his favorite, but I so desired to know his favor. But the more I looked to him, the more I pondered his words, the more I followed his steps and leaned upon his side, the more aware of him I became, and the thoughts of myself and my own concerns became wonderfully lost in that knowledge. The more his life fills me, the less important my life is to me. The joys are beyond what I ever thought I would know; the pains, deeper than I ever thought I could endure. But each struggle has opened my soul and stretched me to both new heights and new depths of knowing Christ."

36

Crucified with Christ

My God, my God, why…?

—MARK 15:34

As we grow closer to any person or object in our lives, our perspective changes, our view brightens, and our understanding increases. As we come closer to Jesus, the same thing occurs. While I am…

in the Crowds, my focus is *my questions;*
in the Five Thousand, my focus is *my needs;*
in the Seventy, my focus is *Jesus' mission;*
in the Twelve, my focus is *his Life;*
in the Three, my focus is *his glory* (and *his sufferings*); but in this closest place of all
in the One, my focus is *Jesus himself,* his presence.

As we come closer and closer to Christ, the events in that final week of Jesus' ministry on earth—the Garden, the cross, the resurrection, and more—serve as a road map of reassurance for us. When we fully follow, we do more than believe in Jesus Christ; we identify with him and correlate the events in our lives with the events in his.

Jesus' life and ministry while on this planet were all about identification—identification with mankind, with you and with me. From his humble manger birth to the wilderness temptations, he identified with our humanness, our struggles, and our weaknesses. As the Bible says, "We don't have a priest who is out of touch with our reality. He's been through weakness and testing, experienced it all—all but the sin" (Heb. 4:15 MSG).

THREE PRAYERS FROM THE CROSS

Against the horrible backdrop of Christ's cross, something glorious stood out like a brilliant diamond against black velvet. The harder Jesus' body was hit with grief and torture, the more radiant his spirit shone, especially in the three prayers he prayed from the cross:

1. "Father, Forgive Them, for They Do Not Know What They Are Doing" (Luke 23:34)

On the cross Jesus displayed *a loving perspective*. Nothing is more loving, or more difficult, than forgiveness. Jesus looked into the faces of his mocking executioners and felt compassion for them. He looked beyond their cursing mouths and saw tongues yet untamed; he looked beyond the pounding of the nails and saw hammer-holding hands yet uncleansed; he looked beyond impassioned anger and saw the hearts he came to save, lives he came to transform.

2. "My God, My God, Why Have You Forsaken Me?" (Mark 15:34)

On the cross Jesus asked *a desperate question* of his heavenly Father, not the question I would have expected from the Son of God. I would have expected something more like the one he asked at Gethsemane—one directed to his disciples—such as, "Why have you men forsaken me? I saved you from sea storms and sickness. Why in my darkest hour of need would you forsake and reject me?"

But Jesus' deepest question was not for the friends around him but for a Father above him. These were the most haunting words Jesus ever spoke: "My God, my God, why have you forsaken me?"

This moment was the climax of Jesus' life of identifying with mankind and humanity's needs, the moment when he fully became all we needed him to be. He not only bore our sins; he became our sins (2 Cor. 5:21) and called on heaven itself to unleash every ounce of punishment we deserved on him, not on us. The most terrifying component of that price was Jesus' vicarious sense of separation from his Father. He identified fully. In those hours he surely felt what we most certainly deserved to feel.

3. "Father, into Your Hands I Commit My Spirit" (Luke 23:46)

On the cross Jesus made *an ultimate decision*. The conflict of the cross was the unprecedented intersection of divinity and humanity. Heaven and hell collided with each other on Calvary, and Jesus was caught in the conflict, enduring it all for our very souls. Yet he found a way to trust his Father through the torment.

"Father, into your hands I commit my spirit." When facing the worst the cross had to offer, Jesus braced himself with incredible trust in his Father's care. When his "spirit" became overwhelmed as he faced death, he committed his spirit to the one who alone could keep him safe and bring him through.

CRUCIFIED WITH CHRIST: WE IDENTIFY WITH HIM

Jesus said our following him would involve a cross of our own: "If anyone would come after me, let him deny himself and take up *his* cross daily and follow me" (Luke 9:23 ESV, emphasis mine).

A. W. Tozer wrote, "One of the reasons we exhibit very little spiritual power is because we are unwilling to accept and experience the fellowship of the Savior's sufferings, which means acceptance of His cross."[1]

In life, there are certain crosses to bear—certain hardships, conflicts, and limitations. There is a big difference, however, between carrying a cross and being crucified on one, and the difference can be summed up in one word: *nails.*

In order to live for God and his purposes, I must first die to myself and my own purposes. In order to be crucified with Christ, I must have three nails pierce my soul to the point of death. *The first nail is forgiveness.* Jesus said, "Father, forgive them for they do not know what they are doing." *The second nail is the nail of mystery.* Jesus said, "My God, my God, why have you forsaken me?" *The third nail is surrender.* C. S. Lewis wrote, "Nothing in you that has not died will ever be raised from the dead."[2]

God used suffering in Christ's life to prepare him to be our Savior; he uses suffering in our lives to prepare us to be his followers! The writer to the Hebrews stated, "He had to be made like his brothers in every respect, so that he might become a merciful and faithful high priest in the service of God, to make propitiation for the sins of the people. For because he himself has suffered when tempted, he is able to help those who are being tempted" (Heb. 2:17–18 ESV).

WHAT KEPT JESUS ON THE CROSS?

Paul said he wanted to be "made conformable" to the death of Jesus (Phil. 3:10 KJV). A closer look reveals Paul was saying he wanted to know and experience the depth of love that would make someone willing to endure a cross, to stay on it out of love. Henri Nouwen provides a key insight here. He helps us see what Jesus was able to muster during his time of prayer at Gethsemane and countless times before:

> Why then could [Jesus] say yes [to the cross]? I can't fully answer that question, except to say that beyond all the abandonment experienced in body and mind Jesus still had a spiritual bond with the one he called Abba. He possessed a trust beyond betrayal, a surrender beyond despair, a love beyond all fears. This intimacy beyond all human intimacies made it possible for Jesus to allow the request to let the cup pass him by become a prayer directed to the one who had called him "My Beloved." Notwithstanding his anguish, that bond of love had not been broken. It couldn't be felt in the body, nor thought through in the mind. But it was there, beyond all feelings and thoughts, and it maintained the communion underneath all disruptions. It was that spiritual sinew, that intimate communion with his Father, that made him hold on to the cup and pray: "My Father, let it be as you, not I, would have it" (Matthew 26:39).[3]

RUSHING TO THE RESURRECTION?

On the cross Jesus completely identified with us and with our needs. That's what the Savior of the world does. Now he calls us to identify with him in his life, his death, and his resurrection. That's what a follower of Christ does.

Too often Christians tend to hurry past the cross and rush to the resurrection. That's understandable but regrettable. The resurrection represents the victory, and all of us love the exhilaration of a victory. But there is so much to consider and experience at the cross. So much we cannot afford to miss. Unless we look long enough at the cross, the resurrection will never mean nearly as much to us as it did to Christ.

Remember . . . in the One, we follow Jesus all the way to the cross, to the place of sacrifice.

37

The One Jesus Loved:
Seven Giveaways

Unless He wanted you, you would not be wanting Him.[1]

—C. S. Lewis

Lincoln is arguably the most admired president in American history. In an interview with Charlie Rose, Doris Kearns Goodwin, a biographer of Lincoln, described the former president's walk and talk: "[The records show that] he walked like a laborer; that he would come home bent over and walking as if he was on tough ground. Some said he walked weirdly. When Lincoln was in the debates with Stephen Douglas, Douglas had a big baritone voice, but Lincoln's was high pitched. This actually proved to help him, because it was [high] it could carry better over the big crowds."[2]

Interestingly enough, some thought it important for us to know the tone and timbre of Lincoln and his voice, yet in all four Gospels we have no record whatsoever of how Jesus walked or the sound of his voice. We don't even have a record of what he looked like for that matter. I am often astounded these biographers chose to leave out such detail. Yet the nature of these narratives was of divine inspiration and origin. With that in mind, we do have scores of Jesus' words and actions, his decisions and associations, and his manner and style.

If I were a private investigator in the first century charged with the responsibility of finding the person who walked the closest with Christ, I believe there would be ample evidence to help me identify just who that person is or was. After years of reading and researching the gospel narratives, I see one figure emerging as Christ's closest disciple. That person: John the Beloved.

Clues That Reveal Christ's Closest Follower

There are several reasons I believe John emerges as the closest follower of Christ:

Clue 1: He Referred to Himself as "the Disciple Whom Jesus Loved"

No less than five times[3] John made reference to himself using not his given name, John, but his spiritual self-description, "the disciple whom Jesus loved." Among all the gospel writers, he was the only one who did so, and yet he is also considered the Apostle of Love or the Beloved Disciple.

Henri Nouwen said it aptly:

We have come to believe in the voices that call us worthless and unlovable. . . .

. . . Self-rejection is the greatest enemy of the spiritual life because it contradicts the sacred voice that declares we are loved. Being the Beloved [of God] expresses the core truth of our existence."[4]

Clue 2: John Leaned His Back upon the Back of Jesus at the Last Supper

John sat the closest to Jesus and comfortably so. During this eventful and emotional last meal together amidst the Passion Week of Christ, John is shown positioned the closest to Christ. The text notes "one of the disciples, the one Jesus loved dearly, was *reclining against him, his head on his shoulder*" (John 13:23 MSG, emphasis mine). The Greek term used here for "reclining" echoes an earlier verse in John's gospel: "No one has ever seen God; the only God, who is *at the Father's side*, he has made him known" (John 1:18 ESV, emphasis mine). So, as John reclined against Jesus' side, Jesus reclined against his Father's.

Clue 3: At the Last Supper John Was the One Peter Asked to Find Out from Jesus Who Would Betray Him

The tension around the table tightened the moment Jesus "became visibly upset, and then he told them why" (John 13:21 MSG). At that moment, Jesus said, "One of you is going to betray me." The disciples "looked around at one another, wondering who on earth he was talking about. . . . Peter motioned to [John] to ask who Jesus might be talking about. So, *being the closest*, he said, 'Master, who?'" (vv. 21–25 MSG, emphasis mine).

If you lack the courage or proximity to ask the source a question, you likely do the next best thing; you ask the person whom you think will be comfortable asking him. That was exactly what Peter did.

Clue 4: He Was the Only Disciple Recorded as
Being Present at Christ's Crucifixion

In his gospel, John recorded he was there standing "near the cross" (John 19:25) along with the three Marys: Jesus' mother, Mary the wife of Clopas, and Mary Magdalene.

As far as we know, John was the only disciple who was an actual eyewitness to Jesus' crucifixion. He was standing close enough to the cross for Jesus to see him (v. 26). He probably watched as the Roman soldiers drove in the nails. If he did, John MacArthur stated, "He surely realized then and there how awful the cup was he had so easily volunteered to drink!"[5]

Clue 5: He Was the Disciple Christ Chose at the Scene
of His Death to Be His Mother's Caregiver

At the cross Jesus made arrangements for the human oversight and caregiving of the two people most personally dear to him. He looked at his mother standing next to John and said, "Woman, here is your son" (v. 26). Then he looked at his Beloved Disciple standing next to Mary and said to him, "Here is your mother" (v. 27). We are told "from that time on, this disciple took her into his home" (v. 27).

Clue 6: He Recorded, and Perhaps Remembered,
More of Jesus' Words than Anyone Else

You could say John was the red-letter gospel writer. In fact, Augustine wrote, "John's Gospel is deep enough for an elephant to swim and shallow enough for a child not to drown."[6] Either John pondered and remembered more of the words of Jesus than did the other gospel writers, or he thought more of them needed to be put in the record.

Howard Ferrin observed, "[Matthew, Mark, and Luke] have given the outward history of the Master; but John presented its inward and eternal meaning. Love is the best interpreter of the

Spirit. The secret of John's deep spiritual insight is love; love is 'full of eyes.' It sees far, far beneath the surface. . . . Love always gives the clearest vision."[7]

Clue 7: He Is the Only Gospel Writer Who Recorded the
  Astounding New Name Jesus Gave to His Followers: Friends

If he had sent it as a formal invitation, it would have looked something like this:

> I no longer call you servants,
> because a servant does not know
> his master's business.
> Instead, I have called you
> friends,
> for everything that I learned
> from my Father I have
> made known to you. . . .
> You are my friends
> if you do what I command.
> (John 15:15, 14)

Oswald Chambers caught something of the wonder of this new way Jesus began to refer to his disciples:

> What is the sign of a friend? Is it that he tells you his secret sorrows? No, it is that he tells you his secret joys. Many people will confide their secret sorrows to you, but the final mark of intimacy is when they share their secret joys with you. Have we ever let God tell us any of His joys? Or are we continually telling God our secrets, leaving Him no time to talk to us? At the beginning of our Christian life we are full of requests to God. But then we find that God wants to get us into an intimate relationship with Himself—to get us

in touch with His purposes. Are we so intimately united to Jesus Christ's idea of prayer—"Your will be done" (Matthew 6:10)—that we catch the secrets of God? What makes God so dear to us is not so much His big blessings to us, but the tiny things, because they show His amazing intimacy with us—He knows every detail of each of our individual lives.[8]

My Longing for the One

John gained the greatest gift we can ever find in this life: Jesus Christ. He was privileged to find a clear view of who Jesus is; he also found a vivid understanding of who he was in the eyes of Christ. John knew. He could tell you. The most important thing about him was that he was "the disciple whom Jesus loved." He used the phrase repeatedly. God loved him; Christ loved him. And just knowing that was life itself.

I don't profess to be the One in God's eyes, but I do confess I want to grow to a place in my relationship with God that, as John, I see myself as "the disciple whom Jesus loves."

The Deep Disciple

Alexander Whyte did quite a bit of investigating into the life of John. He summed up so well the essence of what set John apart from Jesus' earliest followers:

> How did John sink so deep into the unsearchable things of his Master, while all the other disciples stood all their discipleship days on the surface? What was it in John that lifted him so high above Peter, and Thomas, and Philip, and made him first such a disciple, and then such an apostle, of wisdom and of love? For one thing it was his gift and grace of meditation. John listened as none of them listened to all that

his Master said, both in conversation, and in debate, and in discourse. John thought and thought continually on what he saw and heard. The seed fell into good ground. John was one of those happy men, and a prince among them, who have a deep root in themselves.[9]

I am fascinated by the unique life and deep devotion of John the Beloved Disciple. His walk with Christ has captured and recaptured my attention for more than twenty years. There is so much to discover about him that I devoted a full book to focusing on his personal experience of friendship with Jesus: *More than a Savior: When Jesus Calls You Friend*. In that book I wrote,

> Surely arguments could be made that other apostles figured more significantly into the early events of the church. One might consider the zealous preaching of Peter a preeminent trait. Another may cite the theological and church government insights and missionary journeys of Paul as being paramount in their influence. Yet, by virtue of the places he shows up and the passages he penned and remembered, John held a privileged place in proximity to the Master.
>
> Many waxed *bolder*.
> A few even seemed to stand *taller*.
> However, surely none walked *closer*.[10]

While Doris Kearnes Goodwin and Steven Spielberg went to great lengths to retrace the steps and sounds of Lincoln in the film by that name, the gospel writers have done no less for us and so much more. Under the inspiration of the Holy Spirit, they were turned loose to pen the sights, sounds, and insights of the life and ministry of Jesus and of those who surrounded his life. We are given clues into the life and purpose of Christ and of those who found themselves the most caught up in and surrendered to that life. Surely none did more so than "the disciple whom Jesus loved."

Remember ... in the One, we find that one of the best ways to get closer to Christ is to follow the steps of the One who followed him the closest.

38

Risen with Jesus

*The question now is: How do we
drink the cup of salvation?*[1]

—HENRI NOUWEN

One of the most unified groups I have ever been a part of was a citywide roundtable of youth pastors I served with in upstate New York several years ago. After a year or so of monthly meetings that always included doughnuts, coffee, and a great two-hour discussion on some aspect of reaching youth for Christ, we decided to take a bolder step and hold an evangelistic event in our city at the start of the school year. The event would be called Allies, and it was designed with one main goal: to help high school students live out their faith in Jesus more boldly on their respective high school campuses.

The Allies event would be held in a high school auditorium and would be designed to try and bring together every

Christ-following high schooler in our county. The event would include three parts. The first part was a concert with a Christian rock band. The second part was a challenging message from a gifted youth speaker. And the third part was the most unique: we would raise signs that looked like the ones used in national presidential conventions, only instead of bearing the names of states, these had the names of every high school and middle school in our county on them. Once these were raised, the students would be sent to their respective school signs and would have a chance to meet for a few minutes with the other believers from their campus.

Our hopes were that by the end of the night, through the efforts of dozens of area youth pastors, the Christ-following teens of our city would be making plans to share their faith and to hold student-led Bible studies on their campuses. But our dream was suddenly dashed.

The disappointment came in a late Friday afternoon phone call I received from the office of the superintendent of schools telling me we could not hold the Allies event at the high school with which we had signed a rental agreement. The reason was something along the lines of "separation of church and state." By the time that first phone call was over, it appeared that the biggest and boldest outreach dream I had ever had to that point had been dealt a death blow.

My fellow youth leaders and I had been planning Allies for a year. We had carried out countless fund-raisers, created radio ads and posters, and started to mobilize hundreds of youth to attend. But something happened within twenty-four hours of our cancellation call we hadn't expected. The local news media—ABC, CBS, and NBC TV stations and the newspaper—started to cover the story. So, we held our first press conference, and my colaborers in the gospel asked me to read our statement. As I recall, it started out this way: "Two thousand years ago there was Someone else who had no place to lay his head . . ."

Jesus turned the kingdom of common sense on its head in more ways than one. No follower of Christ caught this truth any more vividly than did John the Beloved, the one who uniquely penned, "God is love" (1 John 4:8). Just think of it: to blood-thirsty Zealots Jesus insisted "love your enemies" (Matt. 5:44) and "bless those who persecute you" (Rom. 12:14). To his often-vengeful disciples he upped the tally for required acts of forgiveness from seven to *seventy-seven times* (Matt. 18:22, emphasis mine). And to a bereaved sister named Martha, whose beloved brother, Lazarus (a close friend of Jesus), had just died, he made it clear the resurrection was more than a coming prophetic event:

> "Lord," Martha said to Jesus, "if you had been here, my brother would not have died. But I know that even now God will give you whatever you ask."
>
> Jesus said to her, "Your brother will rise again."
>
> Martha answered, "I know he will rise again in the resurrection at the last day."
>
> Jesus said to her, "I am the resurrection and the life. The one who believes in me will live, even though they die; and whoever lives by believing in me will never die. Do you believe this?" (John 11:21–26)

"I Am the Resurrection"

Into the face of Martha's grief, Jesus came that day. He walked right into her conflict, into her personal cross in life. Her soul was not only wracked by the loss of Lazarus; it was bewildered over the question of *why*. *Why didn't Jesus come earlier? Why did he wait this long?* Surely he could have saved her brother. Martha was struggling with the same thing you and I often struggle with, a nagging *if*—"if you had been here, my brother would not have died" (v. 21). This story is also one uniquely told in John's gospel, the "disciple whom Jesus loved."

What Martha hoped would happen had not. If any present hope was in sight, she could not see it. To Martha's dilemma Jesus brought hope in the form of five short words: "Your brother will rise again" (v. 23). He didn't say *how*. He didn't say *why*. He didn't even say *when*. But he did bring her a promise—and an emphatic one at that.

Martha answered, "I know he [Lazarus] will rise again in the resurrection at the last day" (v. 24). In other words, *I'm familiar with the doctrines. I have studied them well. I know I have the hope of someday seeing my brother again in heaven, in the sweet by-and-by.* It was as if Martha felt for a moment that Jesus was giving her the last thing anyone probably wants at such a moment of deep distress—a Sunday school lesson.

What Martha did not realize, however, is that not only would there one day be a resurrection, but she was at that moment standing directly in front of Resurrection itself, Resurrection incarnate. All the power to resurrect, to bring back to life, to transform, and to make new was in the hands of the one with whom she was at that moment conversing. The dark valley of the shadow of death she had entered just four days earlier was about to be visited by the only person on the planet who possessed a power greater than death. All that was required, Jesus said, was that she "believe."

Certainly Martha's confession of faith in a coming resurrection was no small thing. At least she had a long-term hope in God's ultimate power over death. However, Jesus was calling her to a more immediate awareness, to a personal resurrection.

Resurrection power was not limited to a future event in history. No, resurrection power touched the planet the moment Jesus arrived. Why? Because he was and is and will forever be the "resurrection and the life" (v. 25). Yes, Martha had a hope, but Jesus had a higher one.

THE ROCHESTER TURNAROUND

Over the next few days after our first press conference, the story of the school district shutting down our Allies event was literally the talk of the town. The tension we felt on the planning team soon spread throughout the city of Rochester. It was the number two news story for the entire week. We continued to look for a place to hold our event. We were praying and determined. Best of all, we were unified.

The next day we met with the school board members who were anxious and unsure of what to do. On the one hand, they appeared uncomfortable with an event in their school that would include prayer. On the other hand, they felt equally unsure about telling us no because of our "religious focus" for the event. The other youth pastors and I kept praying and standing our ground that we had a signed contract and hundreds of youth planned to show up.

Before the week was over, the school district decided not to let us use the auditorium that would seat about eight hundred. Instead, the officials referred us to the Rochester Dome Arena that would seat two thousand. By the end of the week, we had probably received fifty-thousand dollars worth of free publicity for our event, seen the event become the talk of the town, and carried out the event with two thousand in attendance, packed to the hilt. Best of all, around two hundred teenagers made commitments to follow Jesus that night.

For most of the students who attended the Allies event, it

was a really good night. For the youth leaders who served on the planning team, it was nothing short of a resurrection!

THE RISEN LIFE

Most of us do just what Martha did; we underestimate the resurrection. We relegate it to the future. And when we do, we miss out on so much purpose and power available to us right here, right now. Of course, the resurrection is a historical and a future event, but it is so much more.

The One who was privileged to walk the closest to Christ, John the apostle, knew this story of Lazarus's resurrection was a critical one to the gospel. It shows that before Jesus resurrected, his resurrection power was at work in the life of one he came to rescue, namely, Lazarus. That not only gave him hope; it also gives us hope. In addition it shows us that the resurrection was not merely a religious historical event or a reason to celebrate Easter. Resurrection is a person and a power, a great power—Jesus Christ himself.

When Peter and John went into the tomb and saw Jesus' body was gone, they had two different reactions. Peter "saw" it was gone, but John's reaction was so significant: "The other disciple [John], who had reached the tomb first, also went in, and he saw *and believed*" (John 20:8 ESV, emphasis mine).

As we grow closer to Christ, our faith in him becomes stronger. As we endure one challenge after another, that same faith becomes more muscular and determined:

> In the Crowds, we experience *hearing faith* as we learn to listen to Jesus.
> In the Five Thousand, we experience *tasting faith* as we receive provision from Jesus.

In the Seventy, we experience *serving faith* as we work with and for Jesus.

In the Twelve, we experience *following faith* as we journey farther with Jesus.

In the Three, we experience *deepening faith* as we learn to suffer with Jesus.

In the One, we experience *overcoming faith* as we depend fully on Jesus.

Each of these experiences in following Christ are all one and the same faith. They are not different faiths. But we joyously find that our faith is a treasure trove of strength and possibilities. Note, however, that our faith is not in faith itself but in Christ. In fact, the strength of your faith is not in its size but in the size of the One in whom it is placed. And without it you cannot please God (Heb. 11).

Remember ... in the One, we find that resurrection
is more than an event we celebrate; it is a person
and a power we experience in our lives.

39

John's Favorite Word

Abide in Me, and I in you.

—John 15:4 nasb

"This is a Crosby Clip," Ed said. "Pastor, have you ever seen one of these?"

Ed was an older man in the church I served in the Boston area. He was retired but had spent most of his life as a bridge-building foreman on highways all over New England. The day he came up to me was within the first few months of my arrival as the new pastor. He said, "I have a gift for you, Pastor."

When Ed handed me the old U-shaped connector bolt, he said, "Pastor, this is a Crosby Clip. And Crosby Clips are used on almost every bridge ever built. And every bridge builder knows that once you attach them, they are not moving one bit. They are fastened to stay. Now, I want you to keep this on your desk, and whenever you feel discouraged or want to leave, just pick it up and remember that through Christ, you will overcome and endure whatever you're facing. Will you do that for me?"

I have held that rough piece of hardware in my hands many times since then, remembered Ed's words, and sensed God renew my determination and remind me of his faithfulness. It is on my desk to this day.

John, the closest follower to Christ, had a Crosby Clip of his own in the form of a word. It was one quite unique to his gospel and one he used repeatedly. And the word?

Abide.

Or to use a similar term we hear more commonly in modern translations of the Bible . . .

Remain.

Remember, when you read the words of John, you are reading the Word of God. Also, however, you are reading the words of Jesus remembered by the one who always referred to himself in his gospel as "the disciple whom Jesus loved." I believe he was the closest disciple to Christ.

John the Beloved not only loved Jesus, but he . . .

followed Jesus,
left all for Jesus,
believed Jesus,
leaned his back against Jesus at the Last Supper,
stood with Jesus on the Mount of Transfiguration,
fell asleep in the Garden of Gethsemane as Jesus prayed
   (not his most glorious moment),
remained, stayed, held tight, yielded, surrendered, depended
   and, yes,
continued to abide in Jesus all the way to the cross and
   beyond.

A. W. Tozer described this practice of abiding that John seemed to so diligently practice as "spiritual receptivity":

Why do some persons "find" God in a way others do not? Why does God manifest His Presence to some and let multitudes of others struggle along in the half-light of imperfect Christian experience? Of course the will of God is the same for all. He has no favorites within His household. All He has ever done for any of His children He will do for all His children. The difference lies not with God but with us. . . .

. . . [What set great saints apart was] *spiritual receptivity*. Something in them was open to heaven, something which urged them Godward. . . . [They] had spiritual awareness and . . . they went on to cultivate it until it became the biggest thing in their lives. They differed from the average person in that when they felt the inward longing *they did something about it*. They acquired the lifelong habit of spiritual response. . . . As David put it neatly, "When thou saidst, Seek ye my face; my heart said unto thee, Thy face, Lord, will I seek."[1]

In a world today so full of options, it is refreshing to meet someone who is committed to friendships, family, marriage, work, and most of all, faith in Jesus. Someone has said that *triumph* is about 10 percent *try* and 90 percent *umph*. In Jewish culture the term *chutzpah* applies. Others would call it *stick-to-itiveness*. The Bible uses words like these:

faithfulness
perseverance
overcome
diligence
pressing on

obedience
remain, or in other words,
abide

ABIDE

John cited Jesus using the word *abide* again and again. John also used it in his letters and narrative. He used his writing brush to paint several aspects of abiding in Jesus.

Abide in God's presence ("house") just as a son with his Father: "A slave does not abide in the house forever, but a son abides forever" (John 8:35 NKJV). The Beloved Disciple, John, referred to God as Father more "than any other inspired writer.... Out of 248 New Testament references to God as Father, John penned 130."[2]

Abide in Jesus as a branch is connected to a vine, the True Vine, and you will bear fruit for God: "Abide in Me, and I in you. As the branch cannot bear fruit of itself unless it abides in the vine, so neither can you unless you abide in Me. I am the vine, you are the branches; he who abides in Me and I in him, he bears much fruit, for apart from Me you can do nothing" (John 15:4–5 NASB).

Abide in your reading, hearing, and studying the Word of God, the Bible: "Jesus said to those Jews who believed Him, 'If you abide in My word, you are My disciples indeed'" (John 8:31 NKJV). John seemed to hear the words and watch the works of Jesus more closely than the other disciples did.

Abide in Jesus and let his words remain in you, and then ask whatever you will of God: "If you abide in Me, and My words abide in you, you will ask what you desire, and it shall be done for you" (John 15:7 NKJV). Now, that's a promise!

Abide in Christ to deter sin: "Whoever abides in Him does not sin. Whoever sins has neither seen Him nor known Him" (1 John 3:6 NKJV).

Abide in love, and you will abide in God: "We have known and believed the love that God has for us. God is love, and he who abides in love abides in God, and God in him" (1 John 4:16 NKJV).

Eugene Peterson paints a vivid picture of the effect of abiding:

> I am the Vine, you are the branches. *When you're joined with me and I with you, the relation intimate and organic, the harvest is sure to be abundant.* Separated, you can't produce a thing. Anyone who separates from me is deadwood, gathered up and thrown on the bonfire. But if you make yourselves at home with me and my words are at home in you, you can be sure that whatever you ask will be listened to and acted upon. This is how my Father shows who he is—when you produce grapes, when you mature as my disciples. (John 15:5–8 MSG, emphasis mine)

THE NEXT NEW THING?

We place a lot of value in today's world on new things and even the next new thing. Sometimes we are prone to do the same when it comes to our growth in God. We may overly value the latest video, blog, seminar, website, or insight. While it is important that our minds and hearts stay open to the fresh *Life*Words God wants to speak over us, it is essential that we "hold fast to that which is good" (1 Thess. 5:21 NASB), that we practice what we have already learned and been taught in our faith journey, and that we abide in Jesus. We are warned against neglecting to do so: "If anyone does not abide in Me, he is thrown away as a branch and dries up; and they gather them, and cast them into the fire and they are burned" (John 15:6 NASB).

It has helped me more than once to take a look at that old Crosby Clip on my desk and remember that Ed said once they are fastened, they aren't moving at all. I know he was reminding me I am supposed to cling tightly to the hand of God and know he is clinging even more firmly to me.

Remember . . . in the One, we find a faith that
always abides, that clings to Christ's words,
his ways, and his will, come what may.

40

John's Best-Kept Secret: The 14:21 Principle

I ... will reveal myself to him.

—JOHN 14:21 WEB

Whom do you trust, I mean, really trust? It is likely that the person you most trust, you will also most entrust with your thoughts, hopes, fears, plans, and even secrets. It seems John was such a person to Christ.

When Jesus sat around the Last Supper table that Thursday night in Jerusalem, he was most certainly aware of whom he could trust and whom he could not. It is interesting to me that he not only dined with a faithful disciple named John; he also ate with one who had already started to betray him and another poised to deny him. It appears he served all of them personally by washing their feet.

It is easy to serve and care for people you trust, but what about those you don't trust at all? Jesus was able, however, to serve and care for people he could *not* possibly trust. He prayed for those who crucified him, even as they were in the process of doing so. But how could he do that? In the sense he was fully God and fully human, how could that fully human part of Jesus serve those guys? Would you? Would I?

The answer, I believe, is that *Jesus did not serve Peter and Judas at the Last Supper and wash their feet based on who they were; he did it based on who he was and is.* In truth, he did it not as unto Peter and Judas but as unto God, unto his Father. It wasn't niceness that caused Jesus to serve them or fear of what they might say if he did not. No, he served them out of obedience to his Father, to his commands and his character and nature.

Jesus knew something. He understood a secret I believe John the Beloved also caught. It is tucked away and hidden in a quotation of Jesus that only John recorded. It is entirely possible that among the disciples John was the only one who remembered it, caught its significance, or thought it worthy of including in his gospel. You have to look closely to see it. It requires study and reflection.

Jesus likely said these words to the disciples at the Last Supper right after identifying a betrayer and a denier in their midst. Jesus said, "Those who accept my commandments and obey them are the ones who love me. And because they love me, my Father will love them. And I will love them and reveal myself to each of them" (John 14:21 NLT).

Did you catch that? The principle is clear. The promise is astounding.

One way to open up this passage is to consider the questions it answers. I believe there are at least four:

1. Who genuinely loves Jesus?
2. How does our love for the Son of God affect his Father?
3. How does Jesus respond to our love?
4. What will result from our obedience to Christ's commands?

Each of these is a blockbuster powerful question that holds eternal and immediate significance. I don't know whether John wrote down these words soon after the Last Supper and years before penning his gospel or whether he pondered them so much he never forgot. Somehow it seems this closest disciple to Christ not only heard Jesus' words that night; he made them his own.

Let's consider these questions one at a time and how Jesus answered them:

1. Who Genuinely Loves Jesus?

Eight words answer this question: "Those who accept my commandments and obey them" (John 14:21 NLT). And what are the commandments of Jesus? He did not add more to the Ten, to the Mosaic law, or to the Jewish Talmud. No, Jesus simplified it for us and said all of them can be summed up in two: " 'Love the Lord your God with all your heart and with all your soul and with all your strength and with all your mind'; and, 'Love your neighbor as yourself' " (Luke 10:27). But he taught of such a love that it is even one that loves its enemies (Matt. 5:43–48).

2. How Does Our Love for the Son of God Affect His Father?

"Because they love me, my Father will love them" (John 14:21 NLT). One of the setbacks of the use of the word *love* in the

English language is that we use it to describe so many different things, from loving hot dogs at the local ballpark to loving people who save our lives—quite a span for one little four-letter word to try to cover.

Although we know God carries a love for the entire world ("for God so loved the world" [John 3:16]), there is a difference between having love for someone and having that person engage your love. This is much like unrequited love in romance. Until we meet the person of our interests, communicate and connect with that one, love is an intent and desire. Once we are engaged, however, a relationship is formed, a connection is made, and intimacy occurs. In the 14:21 Principle, John is telling us that as we engage our love with the Son of God, the Father will further engage his love with us. Have you ever seen a look on a father's face when you did something kind for his son or honored him in some way?

3. How Does Jesus Respond to Our Love?

When we engage Jesus with our love through knowing his commands, obeying them, and engaging him in our lives, we are promised a response. James put it this way: "Draw near to God and He will draw near to you" (James 4:8 NKJV).

You can't do anything to make God love you any more than he does, but there are definitely things you can do to let him love you more. There is a difference between being loved by someone and being in a love relationship with that person. Just consider the two 3:16 verses. The first reads, "For God so loved the world that he gave his one and only Son, that whoever believes in him shall not perish but have eternal life" (John 3:16). God loves by giving us his Son: "By this we know love, that he laid down his life for us, and we ought to lay down our lives for the brothers" (1 John 3:16 ESV). Jesus loves by giving us his life. We love by giving our lives in service to others for Jesus' sake.

4. What Will Result from Our Obedience to Christ's Commands?

This is the secret John discovered and I believe hoped we would discover as we read his gospel: "I will love them and reveal myself to each of them" (John 14:21 NLT). Did you catch that? To the person who loves Christ by accepting his commands and obeying them, Jesus will respond to and engage that love with his own. The relationship we share with him will deepen and continue to grow. But best of all, he promised to "reveal" himself to this kind of follower.

But there's more. When you consider the people who followed Jesus, who walked the closest? Who followed the farthest?

The Crowds listened and saw Jesus from a distance; they *were curious.*

The Five Thousand experienced Jesus' feeding and healings; they *were needy.*

The Seventy served and worked for Christ; they *experienced purpose.*

The Twelve left all and followed Jesus; they *walked with him.*

The Three experienced the heights and depths of Christ; they *suffered and celebrated with him.*

The One, John the Beloved, *obeyed Jesus' command* and *walked with Christ all the way to the cross.*

No, John was not perfect. He experienced fear and hesitation in his journey with Jesus at times. But he is the only one of the Twelve or the Three who is recorded as following Jesus all the way to Calvary, to the cross. And do you remember the promise? "I . . . will reveal myself to him."

It has been said that Jesus' close relationship with the Father empowered him to reveal the Father to others; in that manner, "the Beloved Disciple's close fellowship with Jesus allows that disciple to reveal Jesus."[1]

John was passionate about Jesus, and that is evidenced by his relentless pursuit of him. He noted in his gospel that after hearing that the tomb was empty, he outran Peter to the tomb. At the site, however, Peter went in first. When Peter saw the tomb was empty, we have no record of any particular reaction from him. But John "saw and believed" (John 20:8 ESV). This faithful response to Jesus and his ministry led to a uniquely high privilege.

Oh yes. One more thing: not only did Jesus keep his promise with John to "reveal" himself to him; John was also ultimately privileged to see the revelation of Jesus Christ. When you read that final book of the Bible and see how vividly John was permitted to see Christ in his power and glory, it is nothing short of amazing.

Leonard Sweet wrote, "Following Jesus is just that. It is following *him*. The destination is not the foremost issue. Our future condition is not the issue. Our survival is not even at issue. The focus, the goal, and the reward lie not just in the following but in *whom* we are following. The essence of following is the journey itself—being with Jesus."[2]

John's being given the privilege to be a witness for Jesus is affirmed at the end of his gospel: "This is the disciple who is bearing witness about these things, and who has written these things, and we know that his testimony is true" (21:24 ESV). Because John was privileged to become "the disciple who is bearing witness" by penning the most personal and red-letter gospel of them all and to see the revelation, some commentators contend that God exalted John to a role that superseded that of Peter.

John knew the secret. His relationship with Jesus was one to be desired and from which to learn much; it was also the answer to his mom's prayer. She prayed a bold prayer. Some would say an audacious one. But I believe God saw it as one full of faith and belief. Her prayer and John's obedience were answered above and beyond what they could have ever imagined.

Remember... in the One, we find as we do what Jesus says, he reveals more to us of who he is.

Conclusion
The Relentless Pursuit

At its essence, the Christian life is about following: following Jesus. Intimacy with God is the result of that following. Following is about discovering and digesting Jesus' words, his ways, and his commands. It is about a transformation that comes from becoming more and more familiar with the words and ways of Jesus, but it is about so much more. It is about following Jesus the Man, the Savior, and the Friend. It is about entering into Christ by entering into his words, his works, his joys, and his sorrows. And yet following Jesus is not ever primarily about working harder or praying longer; mostly it is about coming closer to Christ himself.

The Circles of Christ reveal places of proximity in our relationship to the Lord—the Crowds, the Five Thousand, the Seventy, the Twelve, the Three, and the One. To consider these places of privilege is one way to gain a sense of where you are in your journey of following Jesus. And to consider where you are in your faith walk and where God is leading you, it is helpful to study the journeys of those who first followed and especially those who walked the closest with him. In this book, we have walked together through many of those journeys in the Gospels that could also be called the following stories.

Through his words and works in the world today, Jesus is still drawing circles. Circles of Crowds all the way down to Twelves, Threes, and Ones are making their way even closer to Jesus. Regardless of where you find yourself in this journey, I urge you to continue to walk through the Gospels again and again. Every time I do, including the writing of this volume, I find insights and intimacies that are as fresh as a new morning. You will do the same. And remember that in our ongoing walk of faith, we sometimes revisit some of these circles, and when we do, we often find a new depth of appreciation for the disciplines and delights that come within each of them.

The Press of the Relentless Pursuit

Perhaps most amazing is what so many of Jesus' followers surrendered and risked to get closer to this man and follow him. The millions of steps those first followers took to get closer came from an internal fire, a passion, a sense of being called, compelled, and even consumed with the desire to pursue the person of Jesus. You can hear the relentless passion in the words of Paul the apostle:

> Whatever gain I had, I counted as loss for the sake of Christ. Indeed, I count everything as loss because of the surpassing worth of knowing Christ Jesus my Lord. For his sake I have suffered the loss of all things and count them as rubbish, in order that I may gain Christ and be found in him, not having

a righteousness of my own that comes from the law, but that which comes through faith in Christ, the righteousness from God that depends on faith—that I may know him and the power of his resurrection, and may share his sufferings, becoming like him in his death, that by any means possible I may attain the resurrection from the dead. (Phil. 3:7–11 ESV)

Paul revealed in these words his deepest passions. He showed us what kept him moving forward through the struggles, challenges, and sufferings and closer to Jesus in the following journey. In this passage, Paul was determined to "gain Christ." Although his words in Romans make it clear that he never thought he could earn his way into God's grace, it is clear in these words to the Philippians that the discovery of the depths of the person of Christ was an opportunity and pursuit not to be missed. He was undoubtedly determined not to just live through the ups and downs of life but to find Jesus, his help and presence, amid the Gethsemanes and the resurrection experiences of life. Paul was even determined to find something of Jesus in the death he would most certainly soon face as a martyr—"becoming like him in his death." Paul was consumed with Jesus and a life of coming closer to him. He desired the inner circles.

THE PRIVILEGES OF INTIMACY

John became "the disciple whom Jesus loved" not because Christ had only enough love for one of his followers but because Christ had a love that was so wonderful it felt absolutely personal. John caught something most of the other people around Jesus missed—intimacy with God. Other people listened to Jesus, but somehow John listened closer. Other people sat with Jesus, but somehow John sat closer. Other people followed Jesus, but somehow John walked closer. John seemed to embrace moments with Jesus in ways others missed. This tendency shows in the unique intimacies conveyed in his gospel and letters.

Adam and Eve once enjoyed intimacy with God but tragically lost it because of their sin. Jesus came to earth not only to rescue us from our sin and selfishness but also to recapture our ongoing opportunity of intimacy with him, with God the Father, and with the Spirit of God. Yet while God through grace extends the opportunity for recaptured intimacies, he does not force them on us. The words *intimacy* and *force* are diametrically opposed to each other; they don't fit in the same sentence, much less the same heart.

While grace offers the unconditional opportunity to know intimacy with God, this intimacy can be opened and experienced only through our determined and relentless pursuit of the person of Jesus. As Oswald Sanders said, "We are as close to God as we choose to be," and as James affirmed, "Come near to God and he will come near to you" (4:8).

Though grace is unilateral—it is solely the gift of God—the experience of intimacy with God carries a certain reciprocal dynamic. It may be best expressed in the context of a spiritual marriage. Marriage is a revelation or, better said, a series of revelations. And a Christ follower, whether married or single, is greatly helped when he or she discovers how much spiritual union with Christ is like a good marriage. As a matter of fact, Paul the apostle encouraged his readers to make the connection and to ponder it when he said the object lesson of marriage is "a profound mystery" (Eph. 5:32). Let's consider the mystery.

When love captures two hearts, they soon find out there is much to discover. Usually the relationship begins with the first date or two. The revelations begin immediately; the intensities and timetables of disclosure vary, depending on the couple.

All in all, a good marriage occurs when a man and a woman learn how to bare their souls to each other. The union is strengthened when they are able to become melded together into a commitment of ideals shared amid a challenging world of realities. When that happens, intimacy occurs. In like manner, a relationship with God is built upon this process of revelation.

When Jesus promised to "show" himself (John 14:21) to the person who walked in true obedience to him, the Greek word used for "show" was *emphanizo*.[1] This strong word meant he would "exhibit himself in person," "reveal," "disclose his heart through his words," "plainly declare his purpose," and "openly appear" to his obedient follower.

When Jesus made this promise during his most intimate of discourses, it was shocking and profound. To the person who embraced his commands and actually chose to aim his life toward obeying them, Jesus promised to reveal himself. The word used in the New King James Version is *manifest* himself. Note that the promise was not simply to reveal his truth, his will, or more *about* himself but to reveal *himself*. His promise was not universal, but personal; not inclusive, but exclusive.[2]

John the Beloved Disciple, the One, in his journey of faith discovered much more than the duties of obedience to Christ. He unearthed the privileges and intimacies as well. Once he tasted of them he was never the same; nothing else again would ever satisfy him. He tasted and saw just how good God and the Son of God are, and he embarked on a quest that would consume the rest of his life. John caught something that he, his mother, and his brother could not have thought possible—it was not simply a seat close to the throne of Jesus but a most privileged place in his presence, friendship with Jesus. Ultimately, your relentless pursuit will result in rich intimacies with God and the fresh realization that you, too, have become the One Jesus loves.

Acknowledgments

Thank you—

Pamela, for adding so much beauty and joy to my life. No one knows how to embrace moments quite like you.

Kristin, Kara, Kandace, and Rob, our four children, for the ongoing privilege and joy of watching you pursue Christ and his kingdom purpose.

Blythe Daniel, my literary agent, for your vision, your encouragement, and most of all, your enthusiasm.

Kristen Parrish, for tracking with me and helping me keep on course.

Janene MacIvor, for your eye for precision and clarity.

Brian Hampton, for your support of this project.

David Moberg, for that first long phone call and all your patient answers to my questions.

Michael Hyatt, for your passion for writing and for encouraging writers.

David Kopp, for your continued encouragements and belief.

Rick Bloomquist, Del Chittim, Charlie Dawes, Christina Gard, Kent Ingle, John Ortberg, Jeff Sellers, and Josh Minerella, for reading the early drafts and for giving all your input and suggestions.

All my students at Southeastern University, for the high privilege of speaking into your lives and watching you pursue God relentlessly. You guys make going to work so much fun!

My parents, Bob and Beverly Crosby, for sacrificing so much to launch me into life.

My in-laws, Rev. David and Shirley Krist, for teaching me so much about the life of pastoring and ministry.

Rev. Samuel Rodriguez, for your prayers, friendship, and fiery passion for God.

Dr. Robert Cooley and Eileen, for your constant encouragement, steady example, and wise mentoring.

Jason and Hillary DeMeo, Nick and Gina Fatato, and Randy and Becky Young, for sharing such kindred spirits; you guys are family!

Pastors Guillermo and Milagros Aguayo, and your children (Paz, Fe, and Juan-Gui), for making Peru our second home and for your determination to *salvemos a la familia*!

Graciela and Eduardo Lelli, for showing so much excitement about this project when we first met you in Peru of all places!

Dr. Chuck and Peggy Spong, for helping to grow our world of mission and service for the gospel.

Those whom God has privileged me to pastor from New York to New England.

Our prayer team: you know who you are and so does God. You are among our most treasured gifts.

Dawson Trotman and David Watson (God rest their souls), for pursuing Jesus with so much passion and for investing in so many young lives for Christ. You are my heroes in the faith!

Conversation Starters

Below is a list of suggested questions that can be used with a small group, in a one-on-one discipleship or mentoring setting, or privately in prayerful reflection. These will assist you in taking the insights and biblical concepts in this book further in your own spiritual growth and journey in Christ and with his church.

CHAPTER 1: AN OUTRAGEOUS REQUEST

Remember . . . followers of Jesus look for ways to get closer to God.

- Did you ever dream of having an Aladdin's lamp as a kid?
- What would you have wished for then?
- What would you wish for now?

- What do you think about this mom's request of Jesus? What does it seem her motivation was?
- How would you have felt if you were one of the other disciples listening in?
- Did Jesus refuse the mom's request? Explain.
- Have you ever made an "outrageous request" of God? How did it turn out?

The Crowds

Chapter 2: The Rings of the Lord
Remember . . . followers of Jesus refuse to follow at a distance; if you're not moving closer, you're moving away.

- Oswald Sanders wrote, "We are as close to God as we choose to be." Do you think this is true? How so?
- What do you think Jesus meant when he asked James and John, "Can you drink the cup I am going to drink?" (Matt. 20:22).
- Is it ever difficult for you to measure your progress of growing in your Christian faith?
- Is measuring spiritual growth anything like measuring academic development? Explain.
- What are healthy goals of spiritual growth for a Christ follower?
- In which of the six Rings of the Lord do you currently find yourself?
- What would it take for you to get closer to God? What would it require of you?

Chapter 3: Closer
Remember . . . followers want to be only one place—closer.

- What is the biggest thing you've ever asked God for? Are you comfortable sharing that?
- Do our prayers as Christians tend to be "too small," as the quotation from Dawson Trotman asks? How so?
- When in your life have you felt the closest to Christ? Do you remember the time and place? Describe it.
- Which tool would you most likely be inclined to follow in your spiritual development—the Apostles' Creed, the Ten Commandments, or the Lord's Prayer? What about that particular tool do you find helpful or interesting?
- What does it take to cultivate closeness (intimacy) with Christ today?
- What about your life and world get in the way of intimacy with Christ?
- How can you overcome those challenges? What will it take?

Chapter 4: Jesus' POV

Remember ... in the Crowds, we discover how much we need a Shepherd.

- What are some Crowds you recall being a part of?
- Do you have any Crowd memories or stories?
- Have you ever been in a group where something chaotic occurred, like the sheep story in this chapter? Tell about it.
- How does understanding Jesus' POV of you affect your POV of him?
- How has your POV of Jesus changed over the years? What most influenced those changes?
- With which of the "Characteristics of Sheep" do you most identify? How so?
- Does viewing Jesus as your Shepherd help you understand his role in your life? In what ways?

Chapter 5: The Bigger Story

Remember . . . in the Crowds, we follow Christ to the places of watching and listening.

- What is your favorite sports crowd to be a part of? How do you behave when you are there?
- Can Crowds affect or change our behavior? In what ways?
- How long will a person stay in the Crowds before either coming closer to Christ or moving away from him?
- When did you first come into the place of the Crowds in your walk with Christ? Into *the place of watching and listening*?
- What bigger stories do you find yourself drawn toward? What makes them so compelling?
- Have you ever thought of faith as being a part of God's Bigger Story before?
- In what ways is the kingdom of God a bigger story?

Chapter 6: The Day Jesus Followed

Remember . . . in the Crowds, the commotion in our lives has to be cleared so we can hear the words of Jesus.

- Have you ever felt God speaking to you through something a child or young person said? What happened?
- What does the commotion of a crowd look like in your life?
- What are the commotions in your life currently crowding out faith?
- How can you clear the commotion in your life?
- What crowds are in the way of your faith?

- How important are quiet places and stillness to building a strong faith in God? Where do you find these?
- What is one thing you often find pressing in on your heart and mind and crowding out your faith, causing it to diminish instead of strengthen? Worry? Doubt? Disbelief?

Chapter 7: Crowdsurfing: Z's Story

Remember . . . in the Crowds, we have to overcome the obstructions around us so we can get a clearer view of Jesus.

- How do you like the retelling of the gospel in this chapter ("I'm going to leave *my* place. I'm going to come to *your* place. I'm going to take *your* place. Then, we're going back to *my* place," and so on)? Does it resonate with you? How so?
- Can you identify with any of Zacchaeus's challenges? Which ones and how so?
- What do you think about this guy, Z? Like him or dislike him? How so?
- Have you come out of the Crowds and followed Jesus? Have the Crowds come out of you?
- When did you find a Crowd in the way of your spiritual growth?
- What are some things that tend to crowd out your clear view of Jesus?
- What would it be like to have Jesus come to your house?

THE FIVE THOUSAND

Chapter 8: The Day Jesus Wanted to Be Alone

Remember . . . in the Five Thousand, we follow Christ to the places of feeding and healing.

- Have you ever had an experience like the author's, when you misjudged your child too soon? Tell about it.
- How would you describe the way Jesus must have felt at this point of his ministry when he had just learned of the execution of his cousin John the Baptist?
- Do you remember a time when you received difficult news and just wanted to be alone?
- What might it have been like if at that time a crowd showed up and demanded your attention?
- Has there been a time when you found yourself in the Five Thousand, in a time of receiving something from God? What was that experience like? How did it affect you?
- How did Jesus respond to the Five Thousand? What did his response reveal about his character?
- How does Jesus' response to the Five Thousand inform you of the way he looks at you and your needs?

Chapter 9: Sack Lunch Spirituality

Remember . . . in the Five Thousand, we find God can do big things even with our smallest gifts.

- Describe the "perfect sack lunch." What would it include?
- In the story of the Five Thousand, a boy's simple sack lunch was the seed of a miracle. Is there a time you recall God using something small or simple to do something much greater? Tell about it.
- Why do you think Jesus used the boy's lunch that day to begin his miracle? Why not just bring it out of thin air? Wouldn't that have been more impressive?
- What are a few of the interests, skills, or talents that God has given you?

- Is there one of them you have sensed he wants you to use to serve others in ministry? How so?
- What do you have in your hands that God may want to use?
- What will it require of you to put your "sack lunch" in the hands of Christ?

Chapter 10: Something in the Way

Remember . . . in the Five Thousand, *we* are the bread that Jesus takes, blesses, breaks, and gives.

- What is your all-time favorite restaurant? What makes it so good?
- What do you think of the take-bless-break-give sequence in which Jesus handled bread?
- In what ways have you felt God bless the "bread" your life represents?
- In what ways have you felt God break the "bread" your life represents?
- As a Christ follower, what are some things you are starting to learn about the ways of God?
- Dietrich Bonhoeffer wrote, "When Christ calls a man, he bids him come and die." What do you think this means in our lives today?
- How do you tend to deal with broken experiences in your life? Do you see God at work even in them? How so?

Chapter 11: My Kind of King

Remember . . . in the Five Thousand, we are tempted to see Jesus as the king we *want* instead of the one we *need*.

- How about that 24/7 Supernatural Walmart the author mentions? Can you imagine such a place?

- In what ways have you tried to take, make, or force Jesus to do some things in your life?
- What kind of king do you try to turn Jesus into?
- What do you think of the "two Gods" that Tolstoy talked about? Is this true in our lives today?
- Do we tend to try and make God after our image? In what way?
- Is worshiping the God of our own design idolatry? How so?
- What does it really mean to follow Jesus?

Chapter 12: Thinking with Your Stomach

Remember . . . in the Five Thousand, we find that Jesus is the bread and drink we most need.

- Did the author's description of lasagna make you think with your stomach at all? Or what other food item does so the most for you?
- What are your thoughts about this statement from this chapter? "Sometimes the best way to turn our spirits on is to turn our stomachs off, at least for a while."
- Why is fasting such a prominent spiritual discipline in the Bible?
- Is fasting as important today as in Bible days?
- Do we tend to live our Christian faith too much as consumers and not enough as "worshipers"? How so?
- In what way is Jesus the bread we really need?
- In this chapter, Robert Crosby says, ". . . help alone is not enough. It is also important to extend the hope that is found in knowing Christ. People need help and hope. In fact, with hope they will often find themselves empowered to find their own help." Do you agree? Explain.

Chapter 13: Crazy Talk?

Remember . . . in the Five Thousand, Jesus' words and ways may not always make sense to us at first.

- What did you think of the scenario at the start of this chapter about the middle-school-aged daughter?
- Why do you think Jesus moved to using such a raw metaphorical approach at this time in his ministry of the flesh and the blood? What effect did it have on his followers?
- If you had been Jesus' public relations adviser at this point in his ministry, what would you have urged him to do? Why?
- Was all this talk about flesh and blood crazy talk? How so?
- Jesus' words noted in this chapter set the stage for what we now know as the practice or ordinance of Communion. Have we lost something of the raw or prophetic nature of this practice?
- What is the significance of Communion to followers of Christ?
- Do you have a hard time making sense of other things Jesus said or did? What are they?

Chapter 14: LifeWords

Remember . . . in the Five Thousand, we realize what Jesus says are more than mere words; they are Spirit and life.

- Does God's Word ever seem personal or personally directed to you? How so?
- Which verse or passage of Scripture has felt like a *Life*Word to you? In what way?

- What do you think about what Tozer said about the spoken word of God and the written word? Have you ever made this distinction before?
- What makes the Bible extraordinary compared to other books?
- Have you ever experienced a *rhema* word in your life? When and what passage?
- What role does fasting play in helping us hear God's Word?
- What role does God's Word play in your life and walk with Christ?

THE SEVENTY

Chapter 15: Follow, Follow, Follow

Remember . . . in the Seventy, we follow Christ to the places of working and serving.

- Were you more of a "follower" or a "leader" as a child? How so?
- What was Jesus calling us to when he said, "Follow me"?
- How do you answer the question: "Where's your home?"
- How do you answer the question: "Who's your daddy?"
- How do you answer the question: "What's your priority?"
- Have you diminished Jesus in any way as the Dorothy Sayers quotation describes?
- What are some of the more surprising or amazing things you are learning about Jesus?

Chapter 16: Do, for You

Remember . . . in the Seventy, we discover we are not just called to do *something* but to do it for *Someone*.

- Who do people tend to mainly work *for* in their jobs? What motivates their efforts on the job?
- What did the front men do that Jesus sent out "two by two"?
- John the Baptist was a type of "front man" for Jesus. He prepared the way for Jesus. What could we learn from him as followers of Christ?
- What were the roles of these workers?
- Have you yet journeyed into the Seventy? How so?
- This chapter makes the point that "there is a vast difference between *working for* Jesus Christ and *knowing him.*" How would you explain it?
- How does it seem the Seventy got towns and people ready for Jesus' visit? How does their work relate to our work in ministry today?
- Is there something you believe Jesus is sending you out to do? What is it?

Chapter 17: Don't Miss the Wow!

Remember . . . in the Seventy, while we do the work, it is essential for us not to miss the Wow!

- What do you do to pass the time when you are waiting for someone in your family?
- What are some important things around us that we often miss because of being too busy?
- What are some things that make you say, "Wow"?
- Is worship a "Wow" in your life? Explain.
- Why was Jesus disappointed with his disciples' enthusiasm after returning from their mission?
- Does working for God ever tend to remove your sense of worship or wonder? How so?
- With whom do you identify the most—Mary or Martha? In what ways?

Chapter 18: The Locker Room Speech

Remember . . . in the Seventy, we find that Jesus guides us and that his words actually coach us.

- Do you remember any moving locker room speeches in your life?
- What do you think about Coach Brooks's quotation: "When you pull on that jersey, you represent yourself and your teammates. And the name on the front is . . . a lot more important than the one on the back"?
- Do we sometimes wait too long to involve and engage people in ministry? Just how spiritually mature does someone need to be before he can serve in ministry?
- Is ministry just an opportunity we should find for ourselves, or is it something we should actively call people into?
- What would it take for you to travel lighter in ministry? What effect might that have?
- What would it take for you to stay more focused in ministry?
- Are you cultivating faithful ones around you in ministry? How?

Chapter 19: Thank You, George

Remember . . . in the Seventy, we find *the love of power* will harm you but *the power of Love* will free you.

- Are we obsessed with power in our culture today? In what ways?
- When have you felt the most powerful?
- Does your faith in Christ make you feel more or less powerful? How?

- Read Jesus' directive in Matthew 5:38–41. What do you think he meant by this?
- Read Ephesians 3:16–19. How do power and love meet in this passage written by Paul?
- Do you feel the tensions of balancing love and power in your life and world? How?
- Have you ever experienced love overcoming power? When and how?

Chapter 20: We Can Work It Out

Remember . . . in the Seventy, we must work out what God has already worked in.

- What is your favorite place to get a burger?
- Which of these questions have you struggled with the most and how?
  - Is there a God?
  - If so, where is he?
  - And what is he doing right now?

- In what ways do you sense God working in you?
- What experiences have you had thus far trying to work *out* what God has worked *in* you?
- Has finding your ministry and how to do God's will been a struggle for you as it seemed to be for the apostle Paul? How?
- Which metaphor most resonates with you when it comes to working out God's will in your life?
  - Producing a crop?
  - Producing a film?
  - Producing a musical composition?

Chapter 21: *If You've Seen Me*

Remember . . . in the Seventy, we find Jesus came not only to save us but also to show us a perfect Father.

- Did you enjoy the Star Wars movies? Which scene was your favorite?
- Were you surprised when Luke Skywalker found out who his father really was?
- How much of the person you are today is connected to the father who raised you? What was his influence on your life, your nature, and your work?
- Has your earthly father impacted the way you tend to view your heavenly Father? In what ways?
- What did Jesus teach us about
  - the Son of God and his role in our lives?
  - the Spirit of God and his role in our lives?
  - the heavenly Father and his role in our lives?

- When Jesus said, "Whoever has seen me has seen the Father," what does that tell us about God and his nature?
- Read Colossians 1:27. What does this tell us about our relationship with Jesus and with the people in our lives?

THE TWELVE

Chapter 22: *The Following Leader*

Remember . . . in the Twelve, we follow Jesus to the places of leaving all.

- This chapter starts by urging us to pull over to a "rest area" and see where we find ourselves. In which of the places of experiencing Christ do you find yourself most often these days: the Crowds, the Five Thousand, the Seventy, or the Twelve? In what ways?

- Was Jesus a leader or a follower? Explain.
- Much space is devoted in this chapter to defining what Jesus meant when he said, "Follow me." What did he mean when he called us to follow?
- With which of the twelve disciples of Jesus do you most identify? How so?
- Does following something always mean we have to leave something else? What is one thing that following Christ has called you to leave? What was that experience like?
- Do you agree that as Christians today we tend to focus too much on leadership and not enough on following? Does the church most need better leaders or followers? How can you tell?

Chapter 23: Let's Get This Show on the Road

Remember . . . in the Twelve, as we believe in God's Son, his Spirit pours through our lives like rivers.

- Amid a crowd, do you tend to be a shouter, or are you quiet? Do you prefer to talk with a lot of people or just one or two?
- When was a time that Jesus was silent? Why do you think he was so quiet at that time?
- When was a time that Jesus got loud? What purpose did it serve?
- How did Jesus seem to react to people giving him publicity? Why did he respond this way?
- How did you like learning more about the great water-pouring ceremony? Could you picture what this must have been like for the people in those days? Explain.

- What did Jesus mean when he said, "Streams of living water will flow from within" the person who believes? Have you experienced that overflow of God's Spirit in your life? How so?
- What part of your life and experience does God tend to really flow through the most?

Chapter 24: The Gospel According to Peter?

Remember . . . in the Twelve, we find that although God is speaking, sometimes we don't like what he has to say.

- How would you describe Peter? His personality? Do you identify with him? In what ways?
- Who would people you know say Jesus is? Your friends? Family members? Coworkers? Classmates?
- Who does the Bible say Jesus was and is today?
- Who did Peter say Jesus was? How significant a statement was that in his day?
- What were the implications and risks of Peter's confession of Jesus as "the Christ, the Son of the living God"?
- Which of Jesus' promises to Peter most impresses you?
- How do you think the other disciples felt when Peter proceeded to rebuke Jesus? How must Jesus have felt?
- What are the keys of the kingdom and their significance? How did Peter end up using them? How can we use them in our world today?

Chapter 25: The Line Jesus Drew in the Sand

Remember . . . in the Twelve, ordinary people receive an extraordinary call from Christ.

- In what ways were Jesus' disciples ordinary?
- What new boss would want to select an ordinary

leadership team? Why do you think Jesus chose ordinary men instead of extraordinary ones?

- Read the call of Christ in Matthew 16:24. What did Jesus' call require of his followers then? What does it require of us today?
- Which aspects of Christ's call in Matthew 16 do we tend to neglect the most today?
- In what ways is Christ's call to our lives
  - a call to intimacy? What does it mean to be intimate with God?
  - a call to humility? What does it mean to be humble before God?
  - a call to serenity? What does it mean to accept your cross with serenity?
  - a call to loyalty? What does loyalty to Christ look like today?

- What does it take to make Jesus your priority today? What will it cost you to do so?

Chapter 26: The Power of A.S.K.

Remember . . . in the Twelve, we find that following Christ faithfully involves asking him boldly.

- Have you ever learned something about God from a child? Tell about it.
- Have you experienced the power of the A.S.K. experience in prayer? How?
- What things do you tend to ask God for the most? Does that tell you anything about yourself?
- What place did prayer have in Jesus' earthly life and ministry?
- What effect did prayer seem to have on Jesus?

- How would you describe prayer and the place it should play in the life of a Christ follower?
- What is a passion or vision you believe God has placed on your heart? Are you A.S.K.ing God about it? Can we pray about it together right now?

Chapter 27: Get Your Joy On

Remember . . . in the Twelve, the way of Jesus is the way of joy; to follow him is to follow joy.

- Is joy an emotion, an attitude, or a choice?
- What often brings you joy?
- Was Jesus joyful? After all, he was "a man of sorrows" (Isa. 53:3 NASB), right?
- Do you tend to be joyful, or do you have to work at it? How do you work at joy?
- Which of the seven joy-giving disciplines do you practice the most often? Which is one you need to try more often?

  1. reading
  2. singing
  3. giving
  4. communing
  5. meditating
  6. serving
  7. enjoying

- How do you like the C. S. Lewis quotation at the end of this chapter? In order to get your joy on, have you learned how to tell your emotions where to get off? What does it take?

Chapter 28: One in Every Crowd

Remember . . . in the Twelve, we are always doing one of two things: we are *following* or *falling back*.

- What do we know about Judas?
- How would you describe Judas's personality?
- What interactions did Jesus have with Judas that we find in Scripture?
- When do you think Judas and his commitment to Christ fell apart? What could have led to his undoing?
- When have you been tempted to listen more to the Crowds than to Christ?
- Has faith ever been more of an act for you than a relationship? How so?
- What aspects of Judas do you sometimes see in yourself? Are you tempted to be unfaithful or disloyal to Jesus and your faith in him?
- Why do you think Jesus still called Judas friend when he was betrayed and arrested?

THE THREE

Chapter 29: Mama's Prayers

Remember . . . in the Three, we follow Christ to the places of suffering and glory, to the depths and the heights.

- Have you or someone you've known seen the influence of a mother's prayers at work? In what way?
- What did you think of the story of Monica and her son Augustine?
- Which of these experiences of knowing Christ are the most real in your life right now?

- Learning to *listen to Christ*?
- Learning to *receive from Christ*?
- Learning to *work for Christ*?
- Learning to *walk with Christ*?
- Learning to *suffer and reign with Christ*?

- What has been one of the heights you have experienced in life? Did you sense Jesus there with you? In what way?
- What has been one of the depths you have experienced in life? Did you sense Jesus there with you? In what way?
- In what way is it significant that James and John became two of the three closest disciples to Jesus? Was it an answer to prayer?

Chapter 30: Mountain View Lodge

Remember... in the Three, we not only remember the events in Jesus' life; we enter into those events in ours.

- Why do you think Jesus chose Peter, James, and John as the three closest disciples? What did they have in common?
- What was the transfiguration of Christ all about? What was its significance in the life and ministry of Jesus?
- What do you think of Peter's idea to set up three tents on the mountain? What do you think he had in mind? What might have motivated him?
- What is the difference between God's will and God's ways?
- Does it seem Peter sometimes wanted to do God's will *his* way? Do you ever get that way?
- This chapter talks about our identification with Christ. Identifying with Jesus in the events of his life is a great part of our growth in him. In what ways do we experience

- a baptism?
- a transfiguration?
- a crucifixion?
- a resurrection?

- In what ways will we experience an ascension?

Chapter 31: Cloudy Christianity
Remember . . . in the Three, as the clouds around us get darker, we begin to hear God's voice clearer.

- What kind of weather do you prefer: warm, sunny days or cool, cloudy ones?
- What clouds are you currently facing?
- Are clouds a blessing or a curse?
- What do clouds do? How do they affect us?
- If there were no clouds, what would we be missing?
- In what ways is God like a cloud by day or a fire by night in your life?
- "Moses' most intimate times in the presence of God were cloudy experiences." Have you found this to be true in your walk with Christ? How so?
- Are the clouds pushing you away from God or calling you closer to him?
- While you may find it hard to see what lies ahead, do you look more fully to the one who can?
- Did you know that the God of the sun and light also often comes in the clouds?

Chapter 32: Disney's Dynamic Duo
Remember . . . in the Three, we are drawn deeper into the Passion of Christ, into his joys and sorrows.

- What is your favorite Disney film of all time?
- Can you see Disney's Dynamic Duo at work in that film? Or in other Disney Films? How so?
- Do we tend to practice a more shallow version of Christianity today than in the time of the early church? Or even fifty years ago? How so?
- What does it mean to be a deep follower of Jesus?
- What does it mean to know Christ in his sufferings?
- What does it mean to know Christ in his glory?
- How prepared is your faith
  - to be filled with a joy unspeakable? How would you deal with that?
  - to be battered and challenged by struggles and hardships? How would you deal with that?

Chapter 33: Weeping with Christ

Remember . . . in the Three, we come to see our struggles not as difficult events that isolate us from God but as challenges that help us draw closer to him.

- In your experiences of growing in your faith in Christ, have you experienced anything that could be described as
  - *a hearing faith*? How so?
  - *a tasting faith*? In what way?
  - *a serving faith*? Describe it.
  - *a following faith*? How so?
  - *a deepening faith*? In what way?

- Have you experienced any Gethsemanes in your life? How did they affect you and your faith?
- How well are you holding the cup of your life? Or facing the challenges and opportunities that are uniquely yours?

- What kind of stress was Jesus going through in Gethsemane? What weights must he have felt?

Chapter 34: Cowboy Disciple

Remember... in the Three, we become more impressed with the God of power than the power of God.

- Do you know anyone who has the type of personality of Maverick from the movie *Top Gun*? How would you describe him or her?
- How do you think James and John got their nicknames from Jesus of the Sons of Thunder or Thunder Boys?
- When James and John wanted to call down fire from heaven on the Samaritans:
  - What were they thinking? Where did they get such an idea?
  - What kind of a king were they serving?
  - What kind of a kingdom were they building?
  - What does this incident reveal about the will of God and the ways of God?
- Is there a bit of the Cowboy disciple in you? How so?
- Do you tend to *react* or *respond* to challenges?

Chapter 35: Speechless

Remember . . . in the Three, we discover what God desires from his followers is not another speech but an attitude of worship that leaves us speechless.

- Has anything ever left you speechless? Tell us about it.
- Who are two biblical characters you would like to meet for coffee? What would you like to ask them?

- What do you imagine Elijah and Moses talked with Jesus about on the Mount of Transfiguration?
- Of all the characters in the Old Testament, why were Elijah and Moses the two who visited Christ on the mountain? What was their significance to that event and moment?
- What effect does the Father's voice seem to have on this story of the Mount of Transfiguration? What effect does it have on Jesus?
- How does Jesus respond to the various people who spoke to him on the mountain?
  - To Peter?
  - To Moses and Elijah?
  - To the heavenly Father?
- What was the purpose of the Mount of Transfiguration?
- In what ways is our salvation a kind of "transfiguration"?

THE ONE

Chapter 36: Crucified with Christ

Remember . . . in the One, we follow Jesus all the way to the cross, to the place of sacrifice.

- At this point in your faith journey, which of these do you honestly tend to be more focused on?

  1. Your questions
  2. Your needs
  3. Jesus' mission
  4. Jesus' life and its events
  5. Jesus' glory and his sufferings
  6. Or do you focus more on *Jesus himself,* his presence?

- Here are the three prayers Jesus prayed on the cross:

  1. "Father, forgive them, for they do not know what they are doing" (Luke 23:34).
  2. "My God, my God, why have you forsaken me?" (Mark 15:34).
  3. "Father, into your hands I commit my spirit" (Luke 23:46).

- Which of Jesus' three prayers would be the most difficult for you to pray? Explain.
- Which of Jesus' three prayers was the most beautiful? How so?
- What does the cross mean to you? To your life right now? To your past? To your future?
- Do we tend to hurry past the cross and rush to the resurrection? How so?

Chapter 37: The One Jesus Loved: Seven Giveaways

Remember ... in the One, we find that one of the best ways to get closer to Christ is to follow the steps of the One who followed him the closest.

- What are some things you are surprised that we do not know about Jesus from the historical records?
- What are some things you are surprised that we do know about Jesus from the records?
- Which of the clues about the One closest to Christ do you find the most compelling? Explain.
- How was it that only one of the Twelve seemed to make it all the way to the cross? Explain.

- What are some possible reasons that one gospel writer included so many more of Jesus' words than the other three?
- What can you learn from the One closest to Christ that can help you come closer as well?
- What was it that drew Jesus to the One?

Chapter 38: Risen with Jesus

Remember . . . in the One, we find that resurrection is more than an event we celebrate; it is a person and a power we experience in our lives.

- What does it mean to be risen with Christ as a Christ follower? What will it mean in the future? What does it mean right now?
- Which sister do you most identify with as a Christ follower, Mary or Martha? Why?
- Martha was disappointed that Jesus hadn't shown up sooner. Ever felt that way toward God? Explain.
- What does it mean to have *overcoming faith*?
- Is the resurrection
  - an event? How so?
  - an experience? Describe.
  - a power that changes lives? In what ways?
  - a positive attitude? Tell more.
  - a faith booster? How so?
  - Jesus himself? In what way?

- How can a resurrection that happened two thousand years ago bring life to your situation today?

Chapter 39: John's Favorite Word

Remember . . . in the One, we find a faith that always abides, that clings to Christ's words, his ways, and his will, come what may.

- What is your favorite word?
- What was one of John's favorite words?
- How did you like the story about the Crosby Clip? Has an object or emblem given to you ever held similar influence? How so?
- What does it mean to abide as a Christ follower? What does it involve?
- Do you find it difficult or easy to abide in Christ? Explain a bit.
- What aspects of abiding do you most need to work on and develop?
- In what ways did Jesus abide during his earthly ministry?
- Which of Jesus' disciples had the hardest time abiding? How so?

Chapter 40: John's Best-Kept Secret: The 14:21 Principle

Remember . . . in the One, we find as we do what Jesus says, he reveals more to us of who he is.

- What were the tensions and emotional dynamics present at the table during the Last Supper?
- What was the 14:21 Principle that John caught?
- How would you explain it?
- Why did others seem to miss it?
- In what ways might the 14:21 Principle be significant to you in your journey of faith?
- What role does obedience to Christ play in our faith walk and journey?

- What role should love play in our faith walk?
- What do love for God and obedience to him have in common?
- What qualities did John have in his life and faith that you would like to emulate?
- What were some of the responsibilities of faith that John took seriously?
- What privileges did John enjoy?
- Who is "the One Jesus Loves" today?

Notes

Chapter 1: An Outrageous Request

1. R. C. Sproul, *Matthew: St. Andrew's Expositional Commentary* (Wheaton, IL: Crossway, 2013), 500.

2. StudyLight.org, http://www.studylight.org/lex/grk/gwview .cgi?n=4352.

Chapter 2: The Rings of the Lord

1. J. Oswald Sanders, *Enjoying Intimacy with God* (Chicago: Moody Press, 1980), 19–20.

2. A. W. Tozer, *The Pursuit of God* (Camp Hill, PA: Christian Publications, 1982), 12–13.

Chapter 3: Closer

1. C. S. Lewis, *The Collected Letters of C. S. Lewis*, vol. 3, ed. Walter Hooper (New York: HarperCollins, 2007), 119.

2. Robert Foster, *The Navigator: Dawson Trotman* (Colorado Springs: NavPress, 1983), 26.

3. Kevin DeYoung, *The Hole in Our Holiness* (Wheaton, IL: Crossway, 2012), 45.

Chapter 4: Jesus' POV

1. Floyd McClung, *Follow* (Colorado Springs: David C. Cook, 2010), 150–51.

Chapter 5: The Bigger Story

1. By this I don't mean to imply that Jesus or the gospel is ever going to be popular, but it is quite clear in the Gospels that if Twitter or Facebook had been in place in first-century Palestine, Jesus would have been trending at the top for a time at least.

2. Dallas Willard, *Renovation of the Heart* (Colorado Springs: NavPress, 2002), 67–68.

3. R. C. Sproul, *Matthew: St. Andrew's Expositional Commentary* (Wheaton, IL: Crossway, 2013), 186.

Chapter 7: Crowdsurfing: Z's Story

1. [[to come: re: Kent Ingle]]

2. R. Kent Hughes, *Preaching the Word Commentary: Luke*, vol. 2 (Wheaton, IL: Crossway, 1998), 222.

Chapter 10: Something in the Way

1. Michael Card, *The Parable of Joy: Reflections on the Wisdom of the Book of John* (Nashville: Thomas Nelson, 1995), 76.

2. Dietrich Bonhoeffer, *The Cost of Discipleship* (New York: Touchstone, 1959), 89.

Chapter 11: My Kind of King

1. Cited in Aylmer Maude, *Tolstoy and His Problems: Essays by Aylmer Maude* (London: Grant Richards, 1901), 64, emphasis in original.

Chapter 13: Crazy Talk?

1. Michael Card, *The Parable of Joy: Reflections on the Wisdom of the Book of John* (Nashville: Thomas Nelson, 1995), 86–87.

Chapter 14: LifeWords

1. A. W. Tozer, *The Pursuit of God* (Radford, VA: Wilder Publications, 2008), 49–50.

2. See W. E. Vine, *Vine's Complete Expository Dictionary* (Nashville: Thomas Nelson, 1996), s.v. "word," 683.

3. Ibid., emphasis mine.

4. F. F. Bruce, *The Epistle to the Ephesians* (Old Tappan, NJ: Fleming H. Revell, 1961), 131, emphasis mine.

Chapter 15: Follow, Follow, Follow

1. See Luke 10:1. Some versions (including the NIV, NLT, and ESV) cite the number sent out as seventy-two instead of seventy. The KJV and NASB cite seventy. If the number was, in fact, seventy-two, there is the possibility that these disciples were overseen by the twelve apostles. Seventy-two would represent six under the care of each apostle.

2. The words of Christ here are reminiscent of Lot's wife looking back to Sodom and becoming a pillar of salt (Gen. 19:26).

3. Dallas Willard, *Revolution of Character* (Colorado Springs: NavPress, 2002) 14, emphasis in original.

4. Dorothy Sayers, *The Greatest Drama Ever Staged* (London: Hodder and Stoughton, 1938), http://www.gutenberg.ca/ebooks/sayers -greatest/sayers-greatest-00-h.html.

Chapter 16: Do, for You

1. John Calvin, *Institutes of the Christian Religion*, trans. Henry Beveridge (Peabody, MA: Hendrickson, 2008), 449–50.

2. Dallas Willard, *Knowing Christ Today* (New York: HarperCollins, 2009), 142, emphasis in original.

3. Oswald Chambers, *My Utmost for His Highest: An Updated Edition in Today's Language* (Grand Rapids: Discovery House, 1992), January 6.

Chapter 17: Don't Miss the Wow!

1. C. S. Lewis, *Letters to Malcolm: Chiefly on Prayer* (New York: Harcourt Brace Jovanovich, 1964), 93.

Chapter 18: The Locker Room Speech

1. *Miracle*, 2004, directed by Gavin O'Connor, Pop Pop Productions, IMDb.com, http://www.imdb.com/title/tt0349825/trivia?tab=qt&ref_=tt_trv_qu.

2. See, for example, Richard Koch, *The 80/20 Principle* (New York: Doubleday, 2008).

3. John Piper, *Risk Is Right: Better to Lose Your Life than to Waste It* (Wheaton, IL: Crossway, 2013).

4. Carl Lentz, First Thoughts.org, March 29, 2013, http://first-thoughts.org/on/Carl+Lentz/.

Chapter 19: Thank You, George

1. Cited in Steven Englund, *Napoleon: A Political Life* (New York: Scribner, 2004), 298.

2. Cited in Roland Hill, *Lord Acton* (New Haven: Yale University Press, 2000), xxiv.

3. W. E. Vine, *Vine's Complete Expository Dictionary* (Nashville: Thomas Nelson, 1996), s.v. "love," 381–82.

4. See John 21 in *IVP New Testament Commentaries*: "The reference to the Beloved Disciple (vv. 20–23) leads right into an identification of him." BibleGateway.com, http://www.biblegateway.com/resources/commentaries/IVP-NT/John/Later-Disciples-Bear-Witness.

Chapter 20: We Can Work It Out

1. Also see Hebrews 13:20–21.

2. Oswald Chambers, *My Utmost for His Highest* (Grand Rapids: Discovery House, 1992), March 20, emphasis mine.

3. C. S. Lewis, *The Business of Heaven: Daily Readings from C. S. Lewis*, ed. Walter Hooper (San Diego: Harvest Book, 1984), 214.

Chapter 21: If You've Seen Me

1. David Watson, *Called and Committed* (New York: Doubleday Religious Publishing Group, 2000), 188.

2. J. I. Packer, *Knowing God* (Downers Grove, IL: IVP, 1973), 201.

3. Dallas Willard, *Renovation of the Heart* (Colorado Springs: NavPress, 2002), 20.

4. Robert Crosby, *The Teaming Church* (Nashville: Abingdon Press, 2012), 130.

5. Willard, *Renovation of the Heart*, 180.

6. David Platt, *Follow Me* (Carol Stream, IL: Tyndale, 2013), 121.

Chapter 22: The Following Leader

1. Leonard Sweet, *I Am a Follower* (Nashville: Thomas Nelson, 2012), 20.

2. A. B. Bruce, *The Training of the Twelve* (Grand Rapids: Kregel, 1988), 29.

3. Sweet, *I Am a Follower*, 14.

Chapter 23: Let's Get This Show on the Road

1. Zack Eswine, *Sensing Jesus: Life and Ministry as a Human Being* (Wheaton, IL: Crossway, 2013), 245.

2. *The NAS New Testament Greek Lexicon*, s.v. "krazo," http://www.biblestudytools.com/lexicons/greek/nas/krazo.html.

Chapter 24: The Gospel According to Peter?

1. Timothy Keller, *King's Cross* (New York: Dutton, 2011), 20.

2. Alexander Whyte, *Bible Characters in One Volume* (Grand Rapids: Zondervan, 1967), 37–38.

3. Keller, *King's Cross*, 97.

4. R. C. Sproul, *Matthew: St. Andrew's Expositional Commentary* (Wheaton, IL: Crossway, 2013), 500.

Chapter 25: The Line Jesus Drew in the Sand

1. David Watson, *Called and Committed* (New York: Doubleday Religious Publishing Group, 2000), 198.

2. John MacArthur, *Twelve Ordinary Men* (Nashville: Thomas Nelson, 2002), xii.

3. R. C. Sproul, *Matthew: St. Andrew's Expositional Commentary* (Wheaton, IL: Crossway, 2013), 500–501.

4. Francis Chan, *Multiply: Disciples Making Disciples* (Colorado Springs: David C. Cook, 2012), 272.

5. The material in the chapter is adapted from a series of Bible studies and sermons written by Robert Crosby for the American Bible Society. Access the free materials at www.uncover.americanbible.org/uncoverleaders.

6. Watson, *Called and Committed*, 8, emphasis in original.

7. C. S. Lewis, *Mere Christianity*, in *The Complete C. S. Lewis Signature Classics* (New York: HarperCollins, 2007), 175–76.

8. Sproul, *Matthew: St. Andrew's Expositional Commentary*, 501.

9. Timothy Keller, *King's Cross* (New York: Dutton, 2011), 8, emphasis in original.

Chapter 27: Get Your Joy On

1. F. R. Maltby cited in Robert L. Short, *The Gospel According to Dogs* (New York: HarperCollins, 2007), 40.

2. John Piper, *Brothers, We Are Not Professionals: A Plea to Pastors for Radical Ministry* (Nashville: B & H Publishing Group, 2013), 9.

3. C. S. Lewis, *The Complete C. S. Lewis Signature Classics* (New York: HarperCollins, 2007), 117, emphasis mine.

Chapter 28: One in Every Crowd

1. John MacArthur, *Twelve Ordinary Men* (Nashville: Thomas Nelson, 2002), 193.

2. William Tyndale (ca. 1494–1536) is credited with coining this English word *beautiful*. When he translated the Bible into English there was no equivalent word yet in the language, so the word *beautiful* originated in the process of translation. See Andrew Skinner, *A Bible Fit for the Restoration* (Springville, UT: Cedar Fort, 2011), 77.

Chapter 29: Mama's Prayers

1. Henri Nouwen, *Can You Drink the Cup?* (Notre Dame, IN: Ave Maria Press 2006), 116–17.

2. Leonard Sweet, *I Am a Follower* (Nashville: Thomas Nelson, 2012), 208.

3. William Mann, ed., *Augustine's Confessions: Critical Essays* (Lanham, MD: Rowman and Littlefield, 2006), 139.

Chapter 30: Mountain View Lodge

1. Alexander Whyte, *Bible Characters in One Volume* (Grand Rapids: Zondervan, 1967), 40.

2. W. E. Vine, *Vine's Complete Expository Dictionary* (Nashville: Thomas Nelson, 1996), s.v. "transfigure," 639.

Chapter 31: Cloudy Christianity

1. David Watson, *Called and Committed* (New York: Doubleday Religious Publishing Group, 2000), 175.

Chapter 32: Disney's Dynamic Duo

1. David Watson, *Called and Committed* (New York: Doubleday Religious Publishing Group, 2000), 181.

Chapter 33: Weeping with Christ

1. Henri Nouwen, *Can You Drink the Cup?* (Notre Dame, IN: Ave Maria Press, 2006), 28.

2. Ibid., 31, emphasis in original.

3. Ibid., 41.

4. Oswald Chambers, *My Utmost for His Highest* (Grand Rapids: Discovery House, 1992), September 5.

Chapter 34: Cowboy Disciple

1. C. S. Lewis, *Mere Christianity*, in *The Complete C. S. Lewis Signature Classics* (New York: HarperCollins, 2007), 111.

Chapter 36: Crucified with Christ

1. A. W. Tozer, *The Radical Cross* (Camp Hill, PA: WingSpread, 2006), 71.

2. C. S. Lewis, *Mere Christianity*, in *The Complete C. S. Lewis Signature Classics* (New York: HarperCollins, 2007), 177.

3. Henri Nouwen, *Can You Drink the Cup?* (Notre Dame, IN: Ave Maria Press, 2006), 40–41.

Chapter 37: The One Jesus Loved: Seven Giveaways

1. C. S. Lewis, *Letters of C. S. Lewis*, ed. W. H. Lewis (New York: Harcourt Brace Jovanovich, 1966), 412.

2. From interview with Doris Kearns Goodwin by Charlie Rose, November 7, 2012, http://www.charlierose.com/view /interview/12646.

3. John 13:23; 19:26; 20:2; 21:7; and 21:20.

4. Henri Nouwen, *Spiritual Direction: Wisdom for the Long Walk of Faith* (New York: HarperCollins, 2006), 30–31.

5. John MacArthur, *Twelve Ordinary Men* (Nashville: Thomas Nelson, 2002), 114.

6. Attributed to Augustine in Andreas J. Kostenberger, *Encountering John: The Gospel in Historical, Literary, and Theological Perspective* (Grand Rapids: Baker Academic, 2002), 19.

7. Howard W. Ferrin, *Twelve Portraits* (Providence, RI: self-published, 1949), 30–31.

8. Oswald Chambers, *My Utmost for His Highest* (Grand Rapids: Discovery House, 1992), June 3.

9. Alexander Whyte, *Bible Characters in One Volume* (Grand Rapids: Zondervan, 1967), 44.

10. Robert Crosby, *More than a Savior: When Jesus Calls You Friend* (Sisters, OR: Multnomah, 2006), 49–50, emphasis in original.

Chapter 38: Risen with Christ

1. Henri Nouwen, *Can You Drink the Cup?* (Notre Dame, IN: Ave Maria Press, 2006), 102.

Chapter 39: John's Favorite Word

1. A. W. Tozer, *The Pursuit of God* (Camp Hill, PA: Christian Publications, 1982), 66–67, emphasis mine.

2. Beth Moore, *The Beloved Disciple* (Nashville: B & H Publishing, 2003), 135.

Chapter 40: John's Best-Kept Secret: The 14:21 Principle

1. Chris Keith and Larry W. Hurtado, eds., *Jesus among Friends and Enemies* (Grand Rapids: Baker Academic, 2011), 146.

2. Leonard Sweet, *I Am a Follower* (Nashville: Thomas Nelson, 2012), 74, emphasis in original.

Conclusion: The Relentless Pursuit

1. W. E. Vine, *Vine's Complete Expository Dictionary* (Nashville: Thomas Nelson, 1996), s.v. "shew," 570.

2. Adapted from *More than a Savior* by Robert Crosby (Sisters, OR: Multnomah, 1999), 96–98.

About the Author

Robert C. Crosby, D. Min., is a writer, a conference speaker, and a pastor who trains young ministers. He has pastored in Rochester, New York; Boston, Massachusetts; and Dayton, Ohio, and served as a university vice president at Southeastern University. He serves as professor of practical theology at Southeastern in Lakeland, Florida. He and his wife, Pamela, are the founders of Teaming Life and Church Conferences and Resources. They speak at leadership, family life, and church events across the nation and in other countries.

For conference information and event scheduling, contact him at robert.teaminglife@gmail.com.

Connect with Robert Crosby:

www.onejesusloves.com

his website at teaminglife.com

his blog at *Huffington Post*
http://www.huffingtonpost.com/robert-c-crosby-dmin/

his blog at Patheos.com, "Leading the Following Way"
http://www.patheos.com/blogs/robertcrosby/

Facebook: Robert Crosby

Twitter: @rccrosby

You will seek me and find me,
when you seek me with all your heart.
—JEREMIAH 29:13 ESV

Teaming Life Conferences & Resources

with Robert Crosby

Host a

Relentless Pursuit *Event*

in Your Area

Grace is unconditionally given,
*but intimacy with God must be **relentlessly pursued**.*

→ **Catch** the ancient pattern of God calling people from
the Outer Places to the Inner Circles from the Old
Testament to the New.

→ **Experience** great stories of relentless pursuers from the
Bible and church history.

→ **Find** deeper understanding of the beauty of your
friendship with Jesus and pursuing the inner circles.

Schedule an event with
Robert Crosby

Contact us at **robert.teaminglife@gmail.com**

Visit us at **teaminglife.com**

Follow us **@rccrosby**

Teaming Life Conferences & Resources

with Robert Crosby

HOST A

Teaming Church *Event*

IN YOUR AREA

"Robert Crosby's book, The Teaming Church, *is so good,
I had a poster made out of its key ideas and
I am using that with our team and keeping it in my office.
You cannot have a great church without a great team at the core."*
—**John Ortberg, pastor and best-selling author**

→ **Discover** the 7 practices of Teaming Leaders.
→ **Learn** the 5 depths of authentic community and how to
  cultivate more collaborative environments within your
  church or organization.
→ **Catch** the compelling models of the Trinity as "The
  Divine Team" and of the Twelve Jesus chose for his
  personal team.

SCHEDULE AN EVENT WITH
ROBERT CROSBY

Contact us at **robert.teaminglife@gmail.com**

Visit us at **teaminglife.com**

Follow us **@rccrosby**

Teaming Life Conferences & Resources

with Robert and Pamela Crosby

HOST A

Teaming Couples *Event*

IN YOUR AREA

"The Bible says 'these two shall become one.' In God's eyes this union is immediate, but achieving the teaming life in marriage takes time and practice."
Robert and Pamela Crosby

→ **Discover** the inner circles of intimacy in marriage and how they reflect our relationship with Christ.

→ **Learn** the 6 Habits of the Teaming Life and how they will enrich your marriage and family experience.

→ **Catch** the power of "improving your interest rate" in marriage and learn to ask great questions of your spouse.

SCHEDULE AN EVENT WITH
ROBERT AND PAMELA CROSBY

Contact us at **robert.teaminglife@gmail.com**

Visit us at **teaminglife.com**

Follow us **@rccrosby**

Join *The Pursuit!*

The One Jesus Loves

CHURCH RESOURCE PAGE

Free Tools for Your Relentless Pursuit

→ **Sermon Outlines**
→ **Graphs and Visuals** on the Circles of Christ
→ **Small Group** exercises and activities
→ **Videos** with key insights and discussion starters
→ **Interviews** with relentless pursuers

Visit the Resource site at **www.onejesusloves.com**